Green **Line** 5
Das Trainingsbuch

von
Markus Scholz
Johannes Wahl

Klett Lerntraining

Zu diesem Trainingsbuch gehört eine Audio-CD. Mit ihrer Hilfe lernst du, Englisch besser zu verstehen. Die Texte sind im Buch mit dem Symbol gekennzeichnet.

Bildquellennachweis:
Umschlagfoto U1/U4: Cover: Getty Images RF (Digital Vision), München; Seite 110: Fotolia (itsallgood), New York; Fotolia (beeny1983), New York; Fotolia (teracreonte), New York; Fotolia (Helder Sousa), New York; Fotolia (iMAGINE), New York; URW, Hamburg

Sollte es in einem Einzelfall nicht gelungen sein, den korrekten Rechteinhaber ausfindig zu machen, so werden berechtigte Ansprüche selbstverständlich im Rahmen der üblichen Regelungen abgegolten.

Bibliografische Information der Deutschen Nationalbibliothek
Die Deutsche Nationalbibliothek verzeichnet diese Publikation in der Deutschen Nationalbibliografie; detaillierte bibliografische Daten sind im Internet über http://dnb.dnb.de abrufbar.

Sprecherinnen und Sprecher: Dane Askew, Alec Berry, Anna Berry, Kristin Gomes, Katie McCann, Claire Newcomb, Paul Newcomb, Michael Stuchbery, Marie Louise Vollmer, David Walker, Joshua Yates
Produktion: Ton in Ton Medienhaus, Stuttgart

Auflage 4 | 2015

www.klett-lerntraining.de

Redaktion: Sabine Schlimm, Hamburg
Illustrationen: Katja Rau, Fellbach: S. 10, 18, 29, 32, 69, 110, 140
Umschlaggestaltung: Koma Amok, Stuttgart
Satz: DTP-Studio Andrea Eckhardt, Göppingen
Druck: Grafisches Centrum Cuno GmbH & Co. KG, Cuno (Saale)

Printed in Germany
ISBN 978-3-12-949162-1

9 783129 491621

Inhalt

Revision A

Unit 3

Revision B

Unit 4

Lösungen

Zoom-in

Four English-speaking countries

1 Trage die Wörter in die richtigen Felder ein.

Hindi – outback – French-speaking population – apartheid – Bollywood – Aboriginal – Rocky Mountains – Nelson Mandela – platypus – townships – British Columbia – chicken tikka

India	South Africa
______________	______________
______________	______________
______________	______________
Canada	**Australia**
______________	______________
______________	______________
______________	______________

2 *Australia.* Finde im Buchstabengitter die Begriffe, die in die Sätze auf der nächsten Seite gehören.

B	U	F	U	E	D	E	S	T	F	L
O	Z	O	N	E	L	A	Y	E	R	Z
G	A	R	E	L	A	T	I	O	N	S
V	G	C	O	N	T	I	N	E	N	T
E	S	E	T	T	L	E	M	E	N	T
A	I	D	T	G	P	A	Q	O	W	A
W	R	N	T	R	C	A	N	C	E	R

1. The ________________ between white and Aboriginal Australians have always been difficult.
2. Aboriginal families were torn apart during the ________________ and systematic relocation of indigenous people.
3. The Australian ________________ has been completely separated from the rest of the world since about 50 million years ago.
4. You can drive for hours before you reach the next ________________.
5. People are advised not to spend too much time in the sun. If they lie on the beach for hours, they risk getting skin ________________.
6. This is the result of holes in the ________________ ________________.

3 *South Africa.* Ergänze die passenden Begriffe.

poverty – racist – crowded – independence – elections – civil rights – minority – apartheid – president – dominated

Since South Africa's ________________ in 1910 the country had been ________________ by a white ________________. Blacks were seen as second-class citizens *(Bürger)* in the ________________ system. They lived in ________________ in ________________ townships. However, under the ________________ leader Nelson Mandela black South Africans began to fight against the ________________ police state. In the free ________________ after the end of apartheid, Mandela became the first black ________________.

Reading: India's way to independence

A During the 19th century the British founded many colonies. In the year 1900 the British Empire controlled a quarter of the world, from America to Australia, from Asia to Africa. People said that the sun never went down in the Empire, because at any point in time there was always some part on which the sun was shining. One of the most important colonies was India. The British thought that tea and other Indian products were their own and took them to Europe. Just as in South Africa, most native Indians were regarded *(betrachtet)* as second-class citizens *(Bürger)* only, dominated by a wealthy and powerful white minority.

B Mohandas K. Gandhi was born in Gujarat in 1869 as the son of educated and rich parents and was trained in law in London. From there he went to South Africa where he spent the next 21 years (1893–1914) and developed his ideas of non-violence. Here he saw the discrimination of all non-white people. His experience also taught him that only if Muslims and Hindus worked together, they could change the situation.

C However, when Gandhi came back to India after all those years he was a stranger in his own country. As he wanted to learn about the problems of the Indian people he travelled around a lot. Only after he had seen that millions of people lived in poverty, he knew how to challenge the British.

D He asked the Indian people to practise their religion on a certain day. Of course, nobody went to work that day. This general strike was the beginning of his non-violent fight for independence. Later he told the Indians not to buy British products anymore.

E The British government sent him to prison several times. All in all, Gandhi spent eight years in jail. The British hoped that the movement for independence would stop and the Indians would forget about Gandhi. But in the end the British government had to give in and leave India. In 1947 the country became independent.

4 Ordne die Überschriften jeweils einem Textabschnitt zu.

_____ Challenging the British

_____ The final step

_____ India as part of the British Empire

_____ Back home

_____ Gandhi develops his ideas and strategies

5 Sind die folgenden Aussagen *true, false* oder *not in the text*? Kreuze an.

1. The British had colonies on four continents.

☐ true ☐ false ☐ not in the text

2. Ghandi came from a poor background.

☐ true ☐ false ☐ not in the text

3. After his return to India, Ghandi fought for women's rights, too.

☐ true ☐ false ☐ not in the text

4. Ghandi chose non-violent ways to achieve India's independence.

☐ true ☐ false ☐ not in the text

5. A judge sent him to prison for eight years.

☐ true ☐ false ☐ not in the text

6. Muslims and Hindus were unable to form a government for an independent India. So a separate Muslim state was founded: Pakistan.

☐ true ☐ false ☐ not in the text

6 Korrigiere die falschen Sätze.

____

____

____

____

____

____

Listening: Travelling Canada 1

7 Welcher Dialog passt zu welchem Bild?

A: ______________________

B: ______________________

C: ______________________

D: ______________________

8 In welchen Dialogen hörst du die folgenden Wendungen?

1. Don't talk about it. dialogue no. __________
2. Sounds pretty boring to me. dialogue no. __________
3. Oh my God. dialogue no. __________
4. Yeah, that's right. dialogue no. __________
5. Bad luck. dialogue no. __________
6. That's funny. dialogue no. __________
7. (It) is a must-do. dialogue no. __________
8. It was unbelievable. dialogue no. __________

9 Höre dir die Dialoge noch einmal an und beantworte die folgenden Fragen.

Dialogue 1

1. From where do you have a good view of Calgary's skyline?

____

2. How far do the ski jumpers fly?

____

3. What was the name of the hotel?

____

Dialogue 2

4. Who had trouble at Vancouver Airport?

____

5. What was stolen from the car?

____

6. What happened to the girl's brother?

____

Dialogue 3

7. Where did the boy go first?

____

8. Which language did they speak there?

____

9. What did the people do when the bear came?

____

Unit 1

Aspects of Australia

1 Ordne die folgenden Substantive in drei Themenfelder und finde jeweils eine Überschrift dafür.

convict – natural wonder – Oz – penal colony – sunrise tour – prisoner – glass-bottom boat – World Heritage Site – Aussie – criminal – judge – down under – the world's largest coral reef system

2 Übersetze die folgenden Sätze ins Englische.

1. Das Great Barrier Reef gilt als einer der besten Orte zum Tauchen *(diving)*.

2. Der australische Sommer soll sehr heiß sein.

3. Die Beziehung zwischen Aboriginals und weißen Australiern gilt als schwierig.

____

4. Sydney soll sehr schön sein.

____

Feelings

3 Fülle die Lücken mit den angegebenen Verben im *simple past*.

to be in tears – to be lonely – to be so angry – to be scared – to feel bad – to be tired of – to hate – to be glad – to be relaxed – to feel confident

Donna could not believe what she had seen an hour ago. Her boyfriend Justin had again kissed another girl! She ____________________ the arguments with him and ____________________ the idea of meeting him in the evening. While she was thinking about the happy times with him, she ____________________, crying out her frustration. After half an hour her feelings turned into rage. In fact, she ____________________ that she threw his latest present at the wall. Then the doorbell rang. Donna ____________________ that it might be Justin. She ____________________ to see that it was only the postman. When the evening came, she ____________________. Would she ____________________ enough to tell Justin that it was all over? In the end she thought that she had to split up with him. After she had done it, she had mixed feelings. She ____________________ and happy, but she ____________________, too.

Food

4 Löse die Anagramme auf und ordne sie den folgenden Umschreibungen zu.

mymyu – toxice – ibarbe – delevedri

1. delicious ______________________
2. have food brought to your house ______________________
3. from another part of the world ______________________
4. open-air meal with grilled food ______________________

Characterizing people

5 Suche aus der Wortschlange die Adjektive heraus und ordne sie den richtigen Beschreibungen zu.

racistconfidentungratefuldirectaggressiveshyhypocritical

1. to be violent ______________________
2. to think that Aboriginals are second-class people ______________________
3. to know that you can do it ______________________
4. not wanting to thank anybody ______________________
5. honest, straight ______________________
6. to do the opposite of what you tell other people ______________________
7. nervous about speaking to people ______________________

Nouns

6 Wie heißen die entsprechenden Substantive zu den Verben beziehungsweise Adjektiven?

to die:	______	long:	______
to laugh:	______	weak:	______
to move:	______	silent:	______
to examine:	______	amazed:	______

Elements of a story

7 Setze die Begriffe ein und stelle das Lösungswort mit den Buchstaben aus den unterlegten Feldern zusammen.

1. Giving the reader hints how the story might develop

□□□□■□□■□□□□□.

2. Describing the characters

□□■□□□□■□□□□■□□■.

3. Creates false expectations

□□■ □■□■□□□.

4. Most exciting point of the story

□□■□■□.

5. Perspective

■□□□□ ■□ ■□□.

Solution: When students read an English novel, they usually prefer an

□□□□□□□ □□□□□□□.

Used to

Du verwendest ***used to* + Infinitiv**, um auszudrücken, dass in der Vergangenheit gewohnheitsmäßig ein bestimmter Zustand herrschte oder etwas Bestimmtes geschah. Da es sich um etwas Vergangenes handelt, gibt es keine *present-tense*-Form, sondern nur die *past-tense*-Form *used to.*

When I was younger, we **used to** spend our holidays in Italy.
(Als ich jünger war, fuhren wir immer nach Italien in den Urlaub.)

Fragen werden mit *did + use* to gebildet. Die **Verneinung** lautet *didn't use to* oder *never used to.*

What **did** you **use** to play with, grandma?
(Womit hast du früher immer gespielt, Oma?)
I never used to / didn't use to go to the disco when I was your age.
(Ich bin in deinem Alter nie in die Disco gegangen.)

Im Deutschen wird *used to* häufig mit „früher" oder „damals" in Kombination mit „immer" bzw. „nie" übersetzt.

8 Übersetze die folgenden Sätze ins Englische und benutze *used to.*

1. Als Angela jung war, ist sie täglich ihren Großvater besuchen gegangen.

___

2. Vor hundert Jahren kamen die meisten Einwanderer aus Europa.

___

3. Früher bin ich nie gerne ins Theater gegangen, aber heute gehe ich einmal die Woche.

___

4. Was hast du früher eigentlich gemacht, bevor es das Internet gab?

___

English equivalents for „lassen“

Das deutsche Wort „lassen“ kann sowohl „zulassen“ als auch „veranlassen“, „zurücklassen“ oder „belassen“ bedeuten. Im Englischen musst du dafür unterschiedliche Wörter verwenden.

Let
Let bedeutet „zulassen“ bzw. „jemandem etwas erlauben“.
Auf *let* folgt ein direktes Objekt und der Infinitiv ohne *to*.
Linda's parents **let** her go to the party.
(Lindas Eltern erlaubten ihr, zu der Party zu gehen.)

Make
Make mit einem direkten Objekt und Infinitiv bedeutet „veranlassen“ bzw. „jemanden dazu bringen / zwingen, etwas zu tun“.
The principal **made** Kevin apologize to Ben.
(Der Rektor zwang Kevin, sich bei Ben zu entschuldigen.)

To have something done
Du verwendest die Konstruktion *to have* + direktes Objekt + *past participle*, um auszudrücken, dass jemand veranlasst, dass etwas getan wird.
Mrs Barnes **has her** young daughters looked after.
(Mrs Barnes lässt ihre jungen Töchter betreuen.)

Leave
Leave bedeutet „zurücklassen“, „belassen“ bzw. „etwas sein lassen“.
They **left** the door open.
(Sie ließen die Tür offen.)

9 Setze eine Form von *let* oder *make* im *simple past* in die Lücken ein.

1. Tracy's parents ______________ her spend New Year's Eve at Bondi Beach.
2. They ______________ her phone them at midnight.
3. Tracy's mum ______________ her daughter call a taxi to get home safely.
4. Her little sister was disappointed because her parents (not) ______________ her go.
5. Her dad ________________ her stay at home because she was too young.

10 Blake war es zu mühsam, sich um alles für seinen Geburtstag selbst zu kümmern. Schaue dir die Bilder an und beschreibe im *simple past*, was er für sich erledigen ließ. Benutze dabei *have something done*.

1. ________________________________

____

2. ________________________________

____

3. ________________________________

____

Tipp

Achte bei der Konstruktion mit *have something done* darauf, dass das Partizip **nach** dem Objekt steht. Sonst erhältst du eine Form des *present* bzw. *past perfect*:
The teacher **had** the windows **closed**.
(Der Lehrer ließ die Fenster schließen).
Aber: The teacher **had closed** the windows.
(Der Lehrer hatte die Fenster geschlossen).

11 Übersetze die folgenden Sätze ins Englische. Achte darauf, mit welchem englischen Begriff du „lassen“ wiedergibst.

1. Ich glaube, ich habe die Tür offen gelassen.

____.

2. Samstags lässt Papa das Auto waschen.

____.

3. Mama hat mich gestern mein Zimmer aufräumen lassen.

____.

4. Lass Mark in Ruhe!

____.

5. Ich habe meine Tasche in der Schule liegen lassen.

____.

6. Meine Eltern ließen mich nicht gehen.

____.

7. Sie lässt ihre Mathe-Hausaufgaben von ihrem Vater kontrollieren.

____.

8. Lass mich das machen!

____.

9. Der Reiseleiter ließ die Touristen früh aufstehen.

____.

10. Tom ließ sich die ganze Geschichte erzählen.

____.

Defining and non-defining relative clauses

Notwendige Relativsätze *(defining relative clauses)*
- Notwendige Relativsätze geben Informationen, ohne die der Satz nicht verständlich wäre. Sie können nicht weggelassen werden.
- Bei notwendigen Relativsätzen steht im Englischen kein Komma ! Es sollte auch keine Sprechpause entstehen.
  James Cook was the first European **who saw Australia.**
  The first white people **that settled down under** were convicts.

Nicht-notwendige Relativsätze *(non-defining relative clauses)*
- Nicht-notwendige Relativsätze geben eine Zusatzinformation zur Hauptaussage. Man würde die Aussage auch ohne den Relativsatz verstehen, könnte ihn also auch weglassen.
- Nicht-notwendige Relativsätze werden durch Kommas abgetrennt. Damit wird deutlich gemacht, dass es sich um einen Einschub handelt. Die Kommas zeigen außerdem Sprechpausen an.
  Cate Blanchett, **who was born in Melbourne**, won an Oscar for her role in *The Aviator*.
  We started our trip in Canberra, **which is Australia's capital.**

12 Unterstreiche den Relativsatz und setze Kommas, wo sie notwendig sind.

1. The British whose prisons were crowded took convicts to Australia.
2. Many of those who were made to do heavy work in the new colony spent the rest of their lives in Australia.
3. The first free settlers who came to the penal colony arrived in 1793.
4. Up to this day most Australians live on the east coast which Cook discovered first.
5. Place names like Victoria or Queensland which came into use in Queen Victoria's time remind us of Australia's British past.
6. Queen Elisabeth II who is at present the British monarch is also the Queen of Australia.

Relative pronouns

Die **Relativpronomen** leiten Relativsätze ein.
- ***Who*** bezieht sich auf Personen oder Tiere:
  The player **who** wears red is the best.
- ***Which*** steht bei Dingen:
  In the outback, **which** is hot and dry, there is very little traffic.
- ***Whose*** verwendest du bei Besitzverhältnissen bzw. um eine Zugehörigkeit zu Personen und Sachen auszudrücken:
  The temperatures, **whose** extreme differences are often surprising to visitors, range from 5 to over 40 degrees C in July.
- ***That*** kann sowohl bei Personen als auch bei Dingen stehen.
  Es darf nur in notwendigen Relativsätzen verwendet werden !
  Most people **that** spend a longer time at the beach wear T-shirts and caps.

13 Verbinde die Sätze, indem du Relativsätze mit Relativpronomen benutzt.

1. Australia gets very strong sunshine. It has the highest skin cancer rate in the world.

____

____.

2. The huge holes in the ozone layer are a danger to people. People like to spend most of their time outside.

____

____.

3. The skin of people is not adapted to the hot climate in Australia. Their ancestors are from Europe.

____

____.

Contact clauses

Ist das Relativpronomen das **Objekt eines notwendigen Relativsatzes**, kann es weggelassen werden. Man spricht dann von einem *contact clause*.

The Australians **who** we talked to protect themselves against skin cancer.

The Australians we talked to protect themselves against skin cancer.

Aber Achtung: Ist das Relativpronomen das **Subjekt** des notwendigen Relativsatzes, dann ist ein *contact clause* nicht möglich.

The Australians **who** were talking to us like surfing.

14 Setze nur die notwendigen Relativpronomen ein. Wenn du einen *contact clause* bilden kannst, lässt du die Lücke frei.

1. The immigrants ________ used to come from Europe to Australia a hundred years ago almost all come from Asia today.
2. The Aussies ________ I have met more often spend their holidays in Bali or Singapore than in Europe.
3. Their role in the Asian-Pacific world, ________ includes New Zealand and Southeast Asia, has become more important to the Australians.
4. Of course, the people ________ I talked to said that Australia's British background would never be forgotten.
5. The English language, ________ is spoken by almost all Australians, is a daily reminder of their past.
6. The sports ________ most people like are the same as in Britain: rugby and cricket are especially popular.

Reading: Aboriginal culture and history

A Long before white people discovered Australia, Aboriginals had spread across the continent. More than 40,000 years ago they came from Southeast Asia. They moved from one place to another, adapting perfectly to the difficult country and climate. Their famous rock paintings, which are some of the oldest pieces of art in the world, were often used to show other Aboriginal tribes where to find water in very dry areas. Apart from that, these paintings tell of the so-called Dreaming, the beginning of the world.

B There are a lot of stories about the Dreaming, told from one generation of Aboriginals to the next. It is Uluru, the famous rock in the red centre of the continent, which plays an important role in this context. White people call it Ayer's Rock. The Aboriginals believe that in the Dreamtime the land was flat. There were no hills or mountains. One day after heavy rainfalls two boys played in the area and formed the rock out of sand.

C In the eyes of the British, the Aboriginals had no culture at all because they didn't live in real houses and went half-naked. In their racist view the British thought of themselves as better people, having the right to destroy the Aboriginal way of living. There were systematic killings of indigenous people in the 19th century. From 1901 until the 1970s white Australians tried to assimilate the Aboriginals into their white culture. That meant that half-Aboriginal children (i.e. children with one white and one Aboriginal parent) were taken away from their families and educated as whites. These generations of children are called the "Stolen Generations".

D Finally white Australia began to accept the indigenous people. In 1963 Aboriginals received full rights as Australian citizens. In 2008 the Australian Prime Minister Kevin Rudd officially apologized to the Aboriginals for their suffering. The relations between black and white Australians have improved. However, the Aborigines try to keep their own identity alive. The introduction of the Aboriginal flag on National Aborigines' Day in 1971 was quite symbolic of that. The yellow circle (Kreis) in the centre stands for the sun, red symbolises the earth and black the Aboriginals.

15 Ordne die Überschriften jeweils einem Textabschnitt zu.

______ The Aboriginal flag ______ Uluru

______ Rock paintings ______ Violence between whites and Aboriginals

16 Sind die folgenden Aussagen *true, false* oder *not in the text*?

1. The Aboriginals are emigrants from Africa.
   ☐ true ☐ false ☐ not in the text
2. The rock paintings helped Aboriginals to survive in the dry country.
   ☐ true ☐ false ☐ not in the text
3. Only Aboriginal rock paintings tell us about the Dreamtime.
   ☐ true ☐ false ☐ not in the text
4. The Aboriginals believe that at the beginning of time the world was flat.
   ☐ true ☐ false ☐ not in the text
5. The Aboriginals do not like tourists to climb up Uluru.
   ☐ true ☐ false ☐ not in the text
6. The British always showed respect towards Aboriginal culture.
   ☐ true ☐ false ☐ not in the text
7. For more than 60 years half-Aboriginal children were taken away from their families.
   ☐ true ☐ false ☐ not in the text
8. In the 1960s Aboriginals were given the same rights as white Australians.
   ☐ true ☐ false ☐ not in the text
9. There was a long discussion whether to apologize to the Aboriginals.
   ☐ true ☐ false ☐ not in the text
10. The Aboriginal flag has got four colours.
    ☐ true ☐ false ☐ not in the text

17 Bringe die Aussagen in eine zeitliche Reihenfolge, indem du sie nummerierst.

______ White Australia apologized to the Aboriginals.

______ Aboriginals immigrated into Australia.

______ In the Dreaming the earth looked different.

______ The British discovered the Australian continent.

______ Aboriginals were taken away from their families.

______ With rock paintings Aboriginals showed their view of the world.

______ Aboriginals received the same civil rights as white Australians.

______ There were systematic killings of Aboriginals.

Reading: An Australian film

This film (2002) is based on the true story of an Aboriginal woman of the "Stolen Generations". It is set in the 1930s and begins in the small settlement of Jigalong in Western Australia. This outback town lies along the northern part of Australia's 2,000 mile-long rabbit-proof fence, which keeps wild animals off the farmland. Three part-Aboriginal children live with their family in this lonely place in the middle of nowhere. 14-year-old Molly Craig and 8-year-old Daisy Kadibil are sisters. Gracie Fields is their 10-year-old cousin.

In a dramatic scene they are taken away from their mothers and brought by force to the Moore River Settlement north of Perth, a re-education camp where they are supposed to forget their traditions and cultural identity. They have to sleep in a large room offering no privacy. They are not allowed to speak their Aboriginal language, but have to learn English so that they can work as servants to white people.

However, Molly, the strongest of the three girls, can't stand being treated like that. She loves her freedom. One day, while the other children and the white nuns are at church, Molly convinces the other two girls to run away. They want to walk back to their hometown. But not all of them are going to make it.

An Aboriginal tracker *(Spurensucher)* is sent after them to bring them back. Although the girls are well trained in hiding and laying false tracks, the police find out their strategy. When the girls find the rabbit-proof fence they know how to get to Jigalong. For nine weeks they walk along the fence. Strangers help them to survive by giving them food and advice.

However, when they are told that Gracie's mother is waiting for her daughter in the town of Wiluna, the girls split up. Gracie takes the way to the train station in order to go to Wiluna by train. The other two move on, but after a while they turn back to follow their cousin. They arrive at the train station only to see Gracie being caught by the police. They never see her again. Molly and Daisy continue walking along the rabbit-proof fence until they find their home. Together with their mother and grandmother they hide in the desert.

Elements of a story

18 *Title and setting.* Unterstreiche in der Inhaltsangabe des Films alle Informationen zum Setting und schlage einen Titel vor, der sich daraus ergibt.

____

19 *Characterization.* Kreuze an, welche Charaktereigenschaften auf Molly zutreffen. Mehrere Lösungen sind richtig!

- ☐ aggressive
- ☐ clever
- ☐ brave
- ☐ unfair
- ☐ caring about others
- ☐ shy
- ☐ scared
- ☐ racist
- ☐ self-confident
- ☐ ungrateful
- ☐ strong
- ☐ freedom-loving

20 *Turning points and climax.* In welchen Zeilen werden Höhe- und Wendepunkte des Films beschrieben? Finde eine passende Überschrift für die jeweiligen Punkte.

______ ______________________________

______ ______________________________

______ ______________________________

21 *Foreshadowing.* In der Mitte des Textes wird bereits angedeutet, dass Gracie wieder in Gefangenschaft gerät. Schreibe den Satz mit der entsprechenden Zeilenangabe auf.

____

____

Listening: Living in the outback 2

22 Höre dir den Dialog einmal an und trage in die Tabelle ein, welche Argumente für bzw. gegen das Leben im Outback vorgetragen werden.

Pro	Con

23 Höre dir das Gespräch noch einmal an und schreibe auf, was man über die Sprecher erfährt (z. B. Namen, Familien, Wohnorte).

Girl: ____

____

Boy: ____

____

Listening: At the Royal Flying Doctor Service 3

24 Tracy besucht die Station der Flying Doctors in Alice Springs und interviewt den diensthabenden Arzt. Höre dir das Interview an und kreuze die jeweils richtige Antwort an.

1. The service started in

☐ Queensland. ☐ New South Wales.

2. The Flying Doctors care for about

☐ 170,000 people. ☐ 270,000 people.

3. Most of the time the doctors

☐ fly people to the next hospital. ☐ tell people how to help themselves.

4. Every day they fly

☐ 112 people out of the outback. ☐ 150 people out of the outback.

5. To arrive at the place of emergency, it usually takes less than

☐ 45 minutes. ☐ 120 minutes.

6. What does the doctor like about his job?

☐ It is different every day. ☐ You see a lot of the countryside.

Listening: Planning a trip to Australia 4

25 Höre dir das Gespräch im Reisebüro an und zeichne die Reiseroute ein, die vorgeschlagen wird.

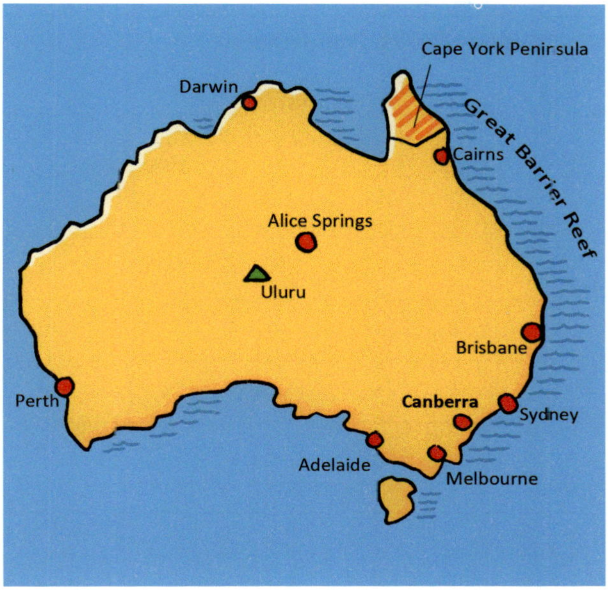

26 Höre dir den Dialog noch einmal an und unterstreiche die richtige Lösung in den folgenden Aussagen.

1. King's Canyon is in the Blue / Green / Red Centre of Australia.
2. The Stuart / the Wellington / the Darwin Highway connects Alice Springs and Darwin.
3. Kakadu National Park is famous for its landscape / its Aboriginal rock paintings / its fun park.
4. The Great Barrier Reef is 2,600 / 2,100 / 2,900 kilometres long.
5. In the Australian winter it is cold / warm / hot in Queensland.
6. Cooktown is west / north / south of Cairns.

Reporting problems to the police 5

27 Höre dir den Dialog auf der Polizeistation an und fülle das unten stehende Formular aus.

Sydney Police Department

Last name: ____________________ First name: ____________________

Street: ________________ City: ________________ Postcode: ________

Date / Time of the crime: ____

Location of the crime: ____

Description: ____

____

____

Writing a postcard

28 Lies dir die Reisenotizen durch und schreibe eine Postkarte nach Hause.

3rd week – Alice Springs – Darwin – Cairns – Great Barrier Reef – diving course – three-day boat trip – reef sharks – cool Aussies on the boat

____

____

____

____

____

____

Apologizing to the Aboriginals

29 In einer viel beachteten Rede entschuldigte sich im Jahre 2008 der australische Premierminister bei den Ureinwohnern. Dabei blickte er auf die Vergangenheit und in die Zukunft. Lies dir den Text auf Seite 23 noch einmal durch und schreibe auf, was er gesagt haben könnte.

Writing a newspaper article 3

30 Höre dir noch einmal das Interview an und schreibe einen Artikel über den Royal Flying Doctor Service für die Schülerzeitung.

Unit 2

Jobs

1 Welche Berufe sind hier abgebildet?

①

②

③

④

⑤

⑥

⑦

⑧

1. ______________________
2. nurse
3. ______________________
4. ______________________
5. ______________________
6. ______________________
7. architect
8. musicen

2 Welche Berufe beschäftigen sich mit den folgenden Dingen?

1. money: Banker
2. education: ____________
3. law: ____________
4. magazines: ____________
5. politics: ____________
6. cakes: Baker
7. food: ____________
8. medicine: ____________

Qualifications

3 Löse das Kreuzworträtsel. Die Buchstaben aus den grau hinterlegten Feldern ergeben als Lösungswort eine der bekanntesten Universitäten Großbritanniens.

Across:
1. place for higher education
2. British qualifications necessary for going to university
3. You take them at the end of your school career.
4. to learn on the job

Down:
5. short form for "General Certificate of Secondary Education"
6. to learn at university

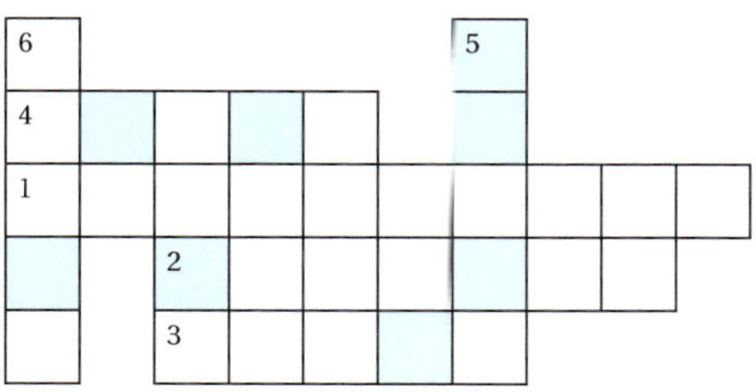

Lösungswort: ___ ___ ___ B ___ ___ ___ ___ ___

The working world

4 Lies den Lückentext und ergänze die passenden Wörter.

personnel manager – placement – the company's website – employer – work experience – deadline – interview – make a good impression – body language – part-time – invitation – competition

If you want to apply for a ______________________, a ______________ ______________ or a full-time job, your letter of application should have no spelling mistakes. As there is a lot of ______________________, a letter with spelling mistakes will be thrown away at once. Sometimes there is a ______________________ so don't be late with your application. If you are lucky, you will get an ______________________ for an ______________________. The ____ will ask you about your qualifications and whether you have got any ____. You should also ask questions about the company. To prepare for the interview, you should check ____.
The interview is very important, so you should try to ____ on the interviewer. He will not only listen to what you're saying but will notice your ____, too. So look confident and smile. The interviewer will not tell you right away whether you have got the job. But perhaps the ______________________ will phone you a couple of days later.

Participles replacing relative clauses

Notwendige Relativsätze kannst du durch Partizipialkonstruktionen ersetzen, wenn das Relativpronomen **Subjekt des Relativsatzes** ist. In den stilistisch eleganteren, formaler wirkenden Partizipialkonstruktionen entfallen das Relativpronomen und ein eventuell vorhandenes Hilfsverb.
Students **who think creatively** could become architects.
→ Students **thinking creatively** could become architects.

Du kannst für solche Konstruktionen entweder das ***present participle*** (*ing*-Form: *going*) oder das ***past participle*** (die dritte Stammform: *gone*) verwenden. Das *present participle* ist eine **aktive Verbform**, ersetzt also **Relativsätze im Aktiv** (mit *simple* wie auch mit *progressive forms*):
Female students **who believe** that construction is a men's world should try a placement first.
→ Female students **believing** that construction is a men's world should try a placement first.

Das ***past participle*** benutzt du, um **Relativsätze im Passiv** zu ersetzen:
Tess looked at the questionnaire, **which had been developed** for teenagers.
→ Tess looked at the questionnaire **developed** for teenagers.

5 Forme die folgenden Relativsätze in Partizipialkonstruktionen um.

1. Only students who have top marks *(Noten)* in their A-levels can go to Oxford or Cambridge University.

____

____

2. Sam took the training course in computer programming which was expected from future IT students.

____

____

3. Parents who are worried about their children's future should talk with them about the pros and cons of their chosen careers.

4. Students who are interested in studying in the USA should look at the universities' websites.

6 Übersetze die folgenden Sätze ins Deutsche.

1. Students wanting information about different career options should go to the Connexions centre.

2. Students invited for an interview should prepare some questions.

3. People who have been out of work for a long time often have difficulties finding a new job.

4. The personnel manager looked at the CV enclosed with the letter of application.

Participles replacing adverbial clauses

Mit adverbialen Nebensätzen kannst du einen Zeitpunkt, einen Grund oder eine Bedingung ausdrücken. **Adverbiale Nebensätze der Zeit** werden häufig durch Konjunktionen wie *when, while* oder *after* eingeleitet. Wenn du Nebensätze der Zeit in Partizipialkonstruktionen umwandelst, entfallen diese Konjunktionen, das Subjekt des Nebensatzes und ein eventuelles Hilfsverb.
When Marco heard that he had passed his A-levels with four As, he dreamt of going to Cambridge University.
→ **Hearing** that he had passed his A-levels with four As, Marco dreamt of going to Cambridge University.

Adverbiale Nebensätze des Grundes werden vielfach mit *because* eingeleitet. In einer entsprechenden Partizipialkonstruktion entfallen diese Konjunktionen ebenso wie das Subjekt und das Hilfsverb.
Tom decided to become a doctor **because he was attracted** by the high pay.
→ **Attracted** by the high pay, Tom decided to become a doctor.

Die Reihenfolge von Haupt- und Nebensatz kann in den Partizipialkonstruktionen meist vertauscht werden, sodass das Partizip durchaus auch am Anfang stehen kann.

7 Ersetze die adverbialen Nebensätze der Zeit durch Partizipialkonstruktionen.

1. When Michael came into the waiting room, he was surprised to see his old girlfriend as a nurse.

____

____

2. He hadn't seen her for a few years while he was studying at York University.

____

____

3. When he looked at her, he didn't know what to say.

____

____

4. While he was standing there, he felt bad.

____

____

8 Formuliere den Text eleganter, indem du die unterstrichenen Nebensätze durch Partizipialkonstruktionen ersetzt. Manchmal ist es besser, die Sätze umzustellen.

<u>When I left school after my GCSEs</u>, I had no idea which career to choose. I did a training course in business <u>because I had to do something</u>. I didn't finish it but it took some time before I found out what I really wanted. <u>While I was working as a waitress</u>, I realized that dealing with people wasn't really my thing. So instead, <u>because I had always felt happy outdoors</u>, I tried a placement with a gardening company. Now I can enjoy the beauty of nature <u>while I am working as a gardener</u>.

____

____

____

____

____

____

____

____

____

____

The perfect participle

Während *present* und *past participle* Gleichzeitigkeit anzeigen, verwendest du das ***perfect participle***, um eindeutig auszudrücken, dass **eine Handlung vor einer anderen** geschah.

Du bildest das ***perfect participle*** mit ***having + past participle***, wenn es Verbformen in aktiven Zusammenhängen ersetzt.
She found talking to the Spanish boy difficult **because she hadn't learned** enough Spanish at school.
→ **Not having learned** enough Spanish at school, she found talking to the Spanish boy very difficult.

Um passive Verbformen zu ersetzen, verwendest du das ***perfect participle passive***: **having + been + past participle.**
After Naomi had been interviewed, she thought she had made a bad impression.
→ **Having been interviewed**, Naomi thought she had made a bad impression.

9 Verbinde die Sätze, indem du eine Konstruktion mit dem *perfect participle* verwendest.

1. The training course had sounded very interesting in the advert. It turned out to be disappointing.

Having sounded

2. I have known what I wanted to do since my 15th birthday. So I am going to apply for a job as a meteorologist tomorrow.

Having known

3. I have been trained as a waiter. Now I want to open a café.

Having been trained

Participle and infinitive after verbs of perception and an object

Nach **Verben der Wahrnehmung** wie *to feel, to hear, to listen to, to notice, to see* und *to watch* kannst du prinzipiell sowohl Partizipien als auch Infinitive verwenden. Beachte aber, dass es dabei einen minimalen Bedeutungsunterschied gibt:

Das ***present participle*** nach einem Verb der Wahrnehmung beschreibt eine **Handlung, die im Moment des Sprechens noch andauert**. Das Ende der Handlung ist noch nicht wahrzunehmen. In dieser Verwendung entspricht das *present participle* der *progressive form*.
We **listened** to Barack Obama **talking** to the American nation.
When Tom had a look at the TV in the pub he **saw** Bayern Munich **defeating** Real Madrid.

Der **Infinitiv** nach einem solchen Verb beschreibt dagegen eine **abgeschlossene Handlung**, die als Ganzes bis zum Ende wahrgenommen werden konnte. Der Infinitiv entspricht hier der *simple form*. In der Regel handelt es sich um Handlungen von kurzer Dauer (z. B. *leave, open*).
I **heard** him **open** the door.
Mary-Sue **watched** her daughter Lynn **say** a polite hello to her new boyfriend.

10 Unterstreiche die richtige Form (Partizip oder Infinitiv).

1. We stopped for a minute and listened to a musician performing / perform a beautiful song.
2. Marco saw Peter working / work in the fish and chips shop when he went by.
3. Blake looked up and suddenly noticed his classmate copying / copy his homework.
4. I watched my little sister dropping / drop her bowl of cornflakes on the floor.
5. He didn't hear the young man saying / say goodbye because he quickly shut the door.
6. When Sue came home she saw her dad sitting / sit in his chair and reading / read the newspaper.
7. Alena watched the thief running / run away until he disappeared around the corner.

11 Deine Mutter ist Zeugin eines Diebstahls geworden. Hilf ihr bei ihrer Aussage bei der Polizei, indem du für sie übersetzt. Achte darauf, ob du Partizipien oder Infinitive benutzen musst!

Police Officer: Let's start at the beginning. You had been waiting at Trafalgar Square for twenty minutes when it happened.
Mutter: Ja, das stimmt. Da war eine riesige Menschenmenge. Ich beobachtete, wie die Menschen kamen und gingen.

Du: Yes, that's right. There was a big ——. I saw the people to came and to go.

Mutter: Ich bemerkte, wie der junge Mann die asiatische Touristin beobachtete. Er saß da und guckte nichts anderes an.

Du: I saw

Police Officer: And then he grabbed the camera, didn't he?
Mutter: Ich habe nicht genau gesehen, wie er die Kamera nahm, weil ich genau in dem Moment woanders hinschaute. Aber ich sah, wie er sehr schnell wegrannte, und hörte die asiatische Frau um Hilfe schreien.

Du:

Police Officer: Okay. Let me write that down …

Going to future and will future

Mit dem ***going to future*** drückst du **Pläne oder Absichten** aus:
Todd is **going to be** a computer scientist.

Das *going to future* ist außerdem die richtige Zeit, wenn schon **Anzeichen** für ein zukünftiges Ereignis zu erkennen sind:
It's ten past nine. We **are never going to get** the train at 9.15.

Das ***will future*** dagegen drückt zukünftiges Geschehen aus, das **unabhängig ist von eigenen Plänen und Absichten.**
The Maths test **will be** on Friday next week.

Du formulierst damit auch Vermutungen oder Erwartungen (nach Wendungen wie *to expect, to be sure* oder *probably*):
I **expect** Jason **will become** a politician. He is good at convincing others.

Außerdem kannst du das *will future* für **spontane Entscheidungen** verwenden, z. B. um Hilfe anzubieten.
I can't finish it until three o'clock. – Okay, I'**ll** give you a hand.

In ***if-Sätzen*** drückst du mit dem ***will future*** eine Folge für die Zukunft aus.
If Wendy wants to be a musician, she **will have to practise** harder.

12 Setze die richtige Futurform ein.

1. I ______________________ (spend) my summer holidays in Italy.
2. Next Saturday I ______________________ (be) 16.
3. Look at the dark clouds. It ______________________ (rain) soon.
4. Derrick ______________________ (probably get) a place at Christ Church College.
5. If I get an A in Maths, Barclay's Bank ______________________ (offer) me a job.

Present progressive and simple present (future sense)

Die Gegenwartszeiten *simple present* und *present progressive* werden im Englischen nur selten benutzt, um Zukünftiges wiederzugeben. Meistens verwendest du *will future* oder *going to future*. In den folgenden Fällen ist das anders:

Das ***simple present*** nimmst du, wenn es um **feste Termine in der Zukunft** geht, auf die du keinen Einfluss hast. Da es sich meistens um genaue Zeitangaben von Fahrplänen und Ähnlichem handelt, nennt man diese Verwendung auch ***timetable future***.
The train to York **leaves** King's Cross at 9.14. So there's still plenty of time.
My interview at the Tourist Office in York **starts** at 12 o'clock.

Das ***present progressive*** verwendest du, um auszudrücken, dass etwas für die **Zukunft fest vereinbart bzw. geplant** ist. In der Regel steht es mit einer konkreten Zeitangabe (z. B. *tomorrow, next week* etc.), damit deutlich wird, dass Zukünftiges gemeint ist.
Danny: What **are you doing** tomorrow afternoon?
Harold: I'**m helping** Olivia with her letter of application.

13 Unterstreiche die richtige Zeitform.

1. Are you coming with us tonight? – No, I watch / am watching the football game on TV at 8.45 pm.
2. The concert begins / is beginning at 7.30 pm.
3. Would you believe it! Mark is taking / takes Sue out for dinner tomorrow night.
4. The plane lands / is landing in Frankfurt at 9.15 am.
5. The train leaves / is leaving Waterloo Station at midnight.
6. Next Sunday Donna helps / is helping her mum prepare the birthday party.
7. Hurry up! The English lesson starts / is starting at 10.30.
8. I go / am going to Paris next weekend.

14 Schreibe auf, was Sean laut seinem stichwortartigen Wochenplan alles vorhat.

Monday:
presentation of History project
Tuesday:
2 pm: have bike repaired at Mario's bike shop
Wednesday:
4 pm: Mum on TV
Thursday:
11.30 am: interview at The Sports Shop
Friday:
7.30 pm: date with Caitlin

15 Setze das Verb in Klammern in die richtige Futurform: *will future, going to future, simple present (future sense), present progressive (future sense).*

Mya: I really don't know what to do after leaving school. But I ______________________ (meet) my personal adviser at the Connexions centre tomorrow.

Megan: I ______________________ (study) at university. I ______________________ (not make) it into Oxford or Cambridge, but perhaps I ______________________ (get) a place at York or Leicester. And then ______________________ (be) a lawyer one day. But anyway, about tonight: What ______________________ (you wear)?

Mya: I thought of my new pink T-shirt.

Megan: Oh, look, I ______________________ (give) you my new ring to wear with it. When shall we meet?

Mya: The train ______________________ (leave) at 7.05 pm. Let's meet at ten to seven.

Megan: You're always late. Tonight probably ______________________ (not be) any different! ______________________ (you please call) me if you aren't on time?

Reading: Differences between Germany and the UK

A The education systems in Germany and the United Kingdom are quite different. While German students have to decide between Hauptschule, (Werk-)Realschule or Gymnasium, most British students go to comprehensive schools *(Gesamtschule)*. So in the UK people with different abilities *(Fähigkeiten)* and various social backgrounds go to the same school.

B In contrast, the German system separates students into three groups. Most children whose parents have themselves had some form of higher education go to Gymnasium, while children with an immigrant background often go to Hauptschule. In no other country in the world is social background said to be that important for your future opportunities in education. However, in a way the pupils' social backgrounds make a difference in the British school system, too. Wealthy children can be sent to very expensive public schools, which are in fact private ones. Those who can afford, for example, to go to a school like Eton are almost sure to get a place at Oxford or Cambridge. For those who cannot afford it, it's much harder to get into these universities.

C Another difference is that in Germany you have to repeat a year if you get bad grades. This is not possible in the UK. If you are not a language whiz-kid, you just go to a lower-level course in French or German. But you will stay with your classmates in your other subjects.

D The role of foreign languages is also quite different. Students attending Realschule or Gymnasium have to learn two foreign languages. They have to take exams in at least one of them. In the UK only 46 % of students take a GCSE in a foreign language. With English as a world language, students do not think it is necessary to learn another language.

E Finally it has to be pointed out that in the UK you have to think much earlier about your career plans. As British students usually only take three to four A-levels, it is an important choice for your future which subjects you choose. If you want to study languages, for example, universities expect you to have good A-level results in them. In contrast to that, in Germany the choice of special subjects *(Leistungs- / Neigungskurse)* does not play such an important role for your future career. With the Abitur German pupils show that they are qualified to study any subject they wish. It is up to the student to fill individual gaps of knowledge *(Wissenslücken)*.

16 Lies den Text durch und ordne die Abschnitte den Überschriften zu.

A Three schools or one for all

D E Languages

E University and career

C Repeating a year

B Students' social backgrounds

17 Sind die folgenden Aussagen *true, false* oder *not in the text*?

1. British public schools are very expensive.
   ☐ true ☐ false ☐ not in the text
2. Eton is one of the most famous public schools.
   ☐ true ☐ false ☐ not in the text
3. For normal students it is not easy to get into Oxford.
   ☐ true ☐ false ☐ not in the text
4. After GCSE most students leave school.
   ☐ true ☐ false ☐ not in the text
5. About 10 % of German students repeat a year in their school career.
   ☐ true ☐ false ☐ not in the text
6. Only 40 % of British students take a GCSE in a foreign language.
   ☐ true ☐ false ☐ not in the text
7. Almost all British students take a GCSE in English.
   ☐ true ☐ false ☐ not in the text
8. Many British students do not think it is necessary to learn a foreign language.
   ☐ true ☐ false ☐ not in the text
9. Which A-level subjects British pupils take depends on their career plans.
   ☐ true ☐ false ☐ not in the text

Reading: Steve Jobs – an unusual career

Steven Paul Jobs was born in San Francisco on February 24, 1955. His parents were two unmarried college students with mixed cultural background. As his mother's family – Catholic immigrants from Switzerland – was against her relationship with his father, a Syrian teacher, the young parents put up their baby for adoption. Steve was adopted by Paul Reinhold Jobs and his wife Clara, an Armenian American. It was Paul who taught his son to work on electronics in the family garage, demonstrating how to take apart radios and television sets and then put them back together again. This became Steve's hobby.

After finishing high school in 1972 he went to Reed College in Portland, Oregon. His parents could hardly afford their son's education so he dropped out of college after a few months. He slept on the floor and returned Coke bottles for money. In 1974 he travelled to India where he stayed for seven months. On his return to the US he had changed his character and his look. He had had his head shaved and wore traditional Indian clothing. He became a Buddhist for the rest of his life.

Steve Jobs started working for Atari, a company which developed computer games. However, two years later Jobs and his friend Steve Wozniak founded their own business in his parents' garage. They called it "Apple Computers Company", a name chosen because it reminded Jobs of a happy summer he had spent picking apples. Wozniak invented the Apple I computer that same year. In the early 1980s Jobs was one of first to realise that the computer mouse would change the world. The mouse-driven Macintosh computer was invented in 1981.

The company grew fast and in 1983 Jobs was successful in hiring John Scully, who had worked for Pepsi-Cola, as managing director (CEO) of Apple. However, two years later Jobs and Scully had several serious arguments about the direction the company should take. Basically they fought about who was the most powerful man in the company. Steve lost the fight and with it his job at Apple. He went on to buy Pixar, a computer animation film studio, for $ 10 million. Over the next 15 years Pixar produced several well-known films including "Toy Story" (1995), "Finding Nemo" (2003), "Ratatouille" (2007) and "Wall-E" (2008), winning the Oscar for "Best Animated Feature" several times.

In 1996 Steve Jobs returned to Apple as the CEO, but the company had almost no money left. With the introduction of the iMac and other new products under his leadership the company was soon successful again.

From 2000 onwards Jobs looked for new areas to make money in. With the introduction of the iPod and iTunes, Apple went into the music business. Finally, with the introduction of the iPhone and its touch display Jobs managed to revolutionize the mobile phone. In August 2011 he had to quit his job: after having been diagnosed with cancer several years before it had become almost impossible for him to work. He died two months later on 5 October 2011.

Steve Jobs earned only $ 1 a year as Apple's CEO, but he held shares *(Aktien)* in Apple and Disney (who had bought Pixar in 2006) worth $ 4.4 billion. The business magazine *Forbes* wrote in 2010 that he was the 42nd wealthiest American. He has been described as the "Father of the Digital Revolution" because his company created completely new technology that we all use today. Without him there would be no computer mouse and no touch screen.

18 Bringe die Aussagen in eine zeitliche Reihenfolge, indem du sie nummerierst.

_____ Steve lost his job at Apple.

_____ He went to India.

_____ He quit his job with Apple.

_____ Steve went to Reed College.

_____ Apple had lost almost all its money.

_____ Steve worked for Atari.

_____ He bought Pixar.

_____ The iPod was invented.

_____ Steve had to sleep on the floor because he had no money.

_____ Apple revolutionized the mobile phone.

19 Kreuze die richtige Antwort an.

1. The person who introduced Steve to the world of electronics was
   - ☐ Steve Wozniak.
   - ☐ his father.
   - ☐ John Scully.
2. Atari is famous for
   - ☐ computer games.
   - ☐ animating films.
   - ☐ its fast computers.
3. Steve founded Apple
   - ☐ in his parents' garage.
   - ☐ in an old factory.
   - ☐ in a newly built megastore.
4. The first Macintosh computer already had
   - ☐ a touch screen.
   - ☐ access to the Internet.
   - ☐ a mouse.
5. Steve and Pixar won Oscars for
   - ☐ Best Male Actor.
   - ☐ Best Animated Feature.
   - ☐ Best Producer.
6. The invention of the iPod went along with
   - ☐ the introduction of the iMac.
   - ☐ the introduction of the iPhone.
   - ☐ the introduction of iTunes.
7. Steve Jobs died at the age of
   - ☐ 55.
   - ☐ 56.
   - ☐ 59.
8. As the CEO of Apple Steve earned
   - ☐ only $1 a year.
   - ☐ $4.4 billion.
   - ☐ $6.2 million.

Reading: Mother Teresa – a career in the name of God

A Mother Teresa was born as Agnes Gonxhe Bojaxhiu in Skopje, Albania on 26 August 1910. She grew up with her sister and her single-parent mother after her father had died when she was 8 years old. From her early childhood Agnes was impressed by stories her parents told about the lives of missionaries. By the age of 12 she was convinced that she should devote her life to God, making the final decision on 15 August 1928 while praying *(beten)* to the Black Madonna of Letnica.

B At the age of 18 she joined the Sisters of Loreto because she wanted to become a missionary. She went away to Ireland to learn English, the language used to teach children in India.

C In 1929 she arrived in India and began teaching at St. Teresa's School in Darjeeling, near the Himalayan mountains. The school was very close to the convent *(Kloster)* of the Sisters of Loreto. This was also the time when she took her first vow as a nun *(Gelübde als Nonne)* and chose the name Teresa. From Darjeeling Mother Teresa went to Calcutta, teaching at St. Mary's High School. She enjoyed teaching but the suffering and poverty outside the convent's walls made a deep impression on her.

D Finally she couldn't stand it any longer and left the convent school in 1948 to help the poorest of the poor. At the beginning there were many difficulties. She had no money at all so she had to beg for food. She suffered from loneliness and thought of going back to the convent. However, she started an open-air school in the slums of Calcutta. It didn't take long before she got the attention of the public, including the Indian prime minister. Volunteers soon joined her in her campaign to help the poor. On 7 October 1950 Mother Teresa left the Sisters of Loreto and founded a new order *(Orden)*, the Missionaries of Charity. The nuns in this order wanted to support the sick and the dying, children without parents, those who had no home, the disabled and the poor.

E Starting with 13 members in Calcutta, the Missionaries of Charity rose to a worldwide organization with more than 4.000 sisters managing hospitals, schools and charity centres in 133 countries on all continents. In 1979 Mother Teresa received the Nobel Peace Prize for her life-long fight against poverty. She didn't want to have the usual formal dinner for the prize winners and asked that the $ 192,000 prize money be given to the poor of India. In Gallup's list of the most admired people of the 20th century she was voted into first place. She died in Calcutta on 5 September 1997, aged 87.

20 Lies den Text einmal durch und entscheide, welche Überschrift zu welchem Textabschnitt passt.

_____ Founding the Missionaries of Charity

_____ The call of God

_____ Teaching in a convent school in Calcutta

_____ Learning English

_____ The Nobel Peace Prize

21 Sind die folgenden Aussagen *true, false* oder *not in the text*?

1. Mother Teresa was born in Calcutta.
   ☐ true ☐ false ☐ not in the text
2. She made her final decision to devote her life to God at the age of 17.
   ☐ true ☐ false ☐ not in the text
3. She joined the Sisters of Charity at the age of 18.
   ☐ true ☐ false ☐ not in the text
4. She became fluent in Albanian, English and Hindi.
   ☐ true ☐ false ☐ not in the text
5. She first taught in a convent school in Madras.
   ☐ true ☐ false ☐ not in the text
6. Mother Teresa was shocked by the poverty around the convent.
   ☐ true ☐ false ☐ not in the text
7. She founded a new order which started with 13 members.
   ☐ true ☐ false ☐ not in the text
8. The Missionaries of Charity care for people with AIDS.
   ☐ true ☐ false ☐ not in the text
9. Mother Teresa built special homes for children without parents.
   ☐ true ☐ false ☐ not in the text

10. She won the Nobel Peace Prize for her support of the disabled.

☐ true ☐ false ☐ not in the text

11. Today the Missionaries of Charity work in more than 120 countries.

☐ true ☐ false ☐ not in the text

12. Mother Teresa has been named 18 times in Gallup's list of the ten most admired women around the world.

☐ true ☐ false ☐ not in the text

22 Korrigiere die falschen Aussagen.

____

____

____

____

____

____

____

23 In welchen Zeilen findest du folgende Informationen?

_____ Agnes' mother told her religious stories.

_____ Agnes started calling herself Teresa.

_____ There was a time in which she was not sure whether she had chosen the right way.

_____ For whom do the Missionaries of Charity care?

_____ Mother Teresa thought that education for the poor was very important.

Listening: Planning a career 6

24 Fülle die Tabelle mit den Berufserfahrungen der beiden Bewerber, ihren Zukunftsvorstellungen und den Vor- und Nachteilen ihrer gewählten Berufe aus.

	Sylvia	Donovan
Work experience (plus comment)		
Career as		
Pros		
Cons		

25 Höre dir den Dialog noch einmal an und kreuze an, wer welche Formulierungen benutzt.

	Sylvia	Donovan
1. To tell you the truth …	☐	☐
2. I don't want to put you off …	☐	☐
3. You've got your head in the clouds.	☐	☐
4. Never mind!	☐	☐
5. Yeah, I know.	☐	☐
6. That's true.	☐	☐
7. Oh, yeah, that's quite annoying.	☐	☐

Listening: Choosing an applicant 7

26 Höre dir die beiden Vorstellungsgespräche für eine Journalistenstelle bei der englischen Zeitung „The Times“ an. Schreibe auf, was der Interviewer nach dem Gespräch an Stärken und Schwächen des jeweiligen Bewerbers notieren könnte.

Interview 1

positive: ______________________________

____

____

____

negative: ______________________________

____

____

____

Interview 2

positive: ______________________________

____

____

____

negative: ______________________________

____

____

____

27 Höre dir die Dialoge noch einmal an und halte fest, wie die beiden Bewerber heißen, wo sie wohnen und wie alt sie sind.

	Applicant 1	Applicant 2
Name		
Address		
Age		

Giving tips

28 Formuliere fünf Tipps für die Bewerber, was sie beim nächsten Bewerbungsgespräch besser machen könnten.

1. ______________________________

____

2. ______________________________

____

3. ______________________________

____

4. ______________________________

____

5. ______________________________

____

Writing: A letter of acceptance

29 Der Personalchef der Zeitung hat sich für einen der Kandidaten entschieden. Schreibe in seinem Namen einen formellen Brief mit der Zusage für die Stelle.

Lea Schmidt
37520 Osterode
Deuts

Applicant's address

Sender's address

Date

Job for redacto

Heading: What is the letter about?

Dear Mr. Pet,

I am writing you

Signature

Enclosures

Writing: Applying for a job

30 Schreibe eine Bewerbung auf folgende Anzeige.

> **Ferienjob an Englands Südküste**
> Das englische Seebad Bournemouth sucht für die Sommermonate deutschsprachige Aushilfen in der Touristeninformation der Stadt. Schicken Sie Ihre Bewerbungsunterlagen in englischer Sprache an:
> **Bournemouth Tourist Information Centre, Westover Rd, Bournemouth, Dorset BH1 2BU, United Kingdom**
> (Allgemeines Abendblatt)

Bournemouth Dorset
BH1 2BU
US
Applicant's address

Bournema
Sender's address

Date

A Application for an assistant
Heading: What is the letter about?

Dear Mr. and Mrs

I am writing for to apply me for your
j

Signature

Enclosures

Tipp

Achte auf einen angemessenen Stil. Zusammengezogene Formen wie „don't" or „I'm" sind in einem formellen Brief nicht üblich. Schreibe stattdessen „do not" bzw. „I am". Ähnliches gilt für andere Abkürzungen und umgangssprachliche Wendungen.

Revision A

Reading: Australia – USA, Australia (2008)

The film “Australia” is a historical romance directed by Baz Luhrmann. It tells the love story between the English Lady Sarah Ashley (Nicole Kidman) and an Australian cattle drover *(Viehtreiber)* called Drover (Hugh Jackman). The story is set in the Northern Territory during World War II.

Lady Ashley’s husband has built the farm Faraway Downs in the Australian outback and plans to bring 1,500 cattle to Darwin to support the army. However, at the beginning of the film he is murdered by King Carney’s men, who want to end the competition in the cattle business. Although Lady Ashley has no experience in farming or business, she decides to continue her husband’s work with the help of Drover and the boy Nullah (Brandon Walters). Nullah is of mixed race, having a white father and an Aboriginal mother. In those days part-Aboriginal children were often taken away from their parents to be educated in a white environment. Nullah therefore lives in danger of being found by the police. When Nullah’s mother dies while hiding from the authorities *(Behörden, Polizei)*, Lady Ashley begins to treat the boy as her own son. She tries to bring the cattle to Darwin in place of her late *(verstorben)* husband. With the help of a handful of people she manages to reach the town with her cattle, although King Carney tries to stop her.

On their adventurous trip to Darwin Lady Ashley and Drover fall in love and she asks him to stay at Faraway Downs. Loving his freedom and independence, he lives there for half of the year, spending the rest of the time driving cattle. Although they do not marry, they form a family with Nullah until one day the lovers have a serious argument and Drover leaves.

The war reaches Australia in 1942 and King Carney’s son-in-law has Nullah taken away by the police to an island north of Darwin where there is a missionary station for Aboriginal children of mixed race. When the town is attacked and destroyed by the Japanese in February of the same year, Drover returns from a period of separation *(Trennung)*. He rescues the boy and they reunite *(wiedervereinigen)* with Lady Ashley for a happy ending.

The film successfully mixes a love story with historical background. However, the story does not only deal with Australia's experiences during World War II. Luhrmann does a good job of introducing the topic of the "Stolen Generations" by including the half-Aboriginal boy. Nullah is brilliantly played by 12-year-old Brandon Walters who won the Australian Critics Award as Best Supporting Actor. Together with him, Australian-born Nicole Kidman and Hugh Jackman – both of them convincing in their roles – make this a romantic and highly entertaining film.

Above all, "Australia" is a love letter to the Australian landscape. The scenes of the outback are breathtaking. One should also mention the costumes that were not only well-designed but also historically correct. It was for good reasons that the costume designer was nominated for an Oscar. However, with its 165 minutes the film is far too long. Especially in the first two hours it has trouble developing a convincing plot. Although it is never truly boring, some parts could have been shortened. All in all, although perhaps not a brilliant piece of art, it certainly is an impressive and important film about and for Australia. It is definitely recommended for travellers and fans of the country.

★ ★ ★ ★ ☆

1 Kreuze an, um was für eine Textsorte es sich handelt.

☐ part of a novel ☐ film review ☐ newspaper report

2 Vervollständige die Tabelle.

Title:			
Category:			
Running time:		Year:	
Director:			
Cast: (actors / role)			
Awards: (nominations and wins)			
Rating in the review:			

3 Kreuze bei den Sätzen unten an, ob es sich um Tatsachen oder die Meinung des Kritikers handelt.

1. The film is set in Darwin and the outback of the Northern Territory.
   ☐ fact ☐ opinion
2. Nullah belongs to the "Stolen Generations".
   ☐ fact ☐ opinion
3. Drover loves his freedom and independence.
   ☐ fact ☐ opinion
4. All major actors are convincing.
   ☐ fact ☐ opinion
5. The film is far too long.
   ☐ fact ☐ opinion
6. Nicole Kidman was born in Australia.
   ☐ fact ☐ opinion
7. Love story and historical background are put together very well.
   ☐ fact ☐ opinion
8. The pictures of the outback are breathtaking.
   ☐ fact ☐ opinion
9. The love story has a happy ending.
   ☐ fact ☐ opinion

4 Unterstreiche die richtige Lösung.

1. The film was produced in the USA and Australia / New Zealand / Canada.
2. Lady Ashley's farm is called Faraway Downs / Middle of nowhere / Lonely River.
3. King Carney is fair / unfair to Lady Ashley.
4. The plot ends in the year 1939 / 1942 / 1945.
5. The story is romantic / sad / driven by action.

Mediation: Am I qualified for the job?

5 Dein englischer Freund Todd hat eine Stellenanzeige entdeckt. Fasse die wichtigsten Informationen zum Unternehmen, zu den angegebenen Qualifikationen und den Fähigkeiten des Bewerbers bzw. den Stellenanforderungen für ihn in einer E-Mail zusammen.

Projektmanager(in)

Wir sind ein weltweit operierendes Unternehmen mit 10 Standorten auf 4 Kontinenten. Wir beliefern alle führenden Automobil-Unternehmen, sodass unsere Elektronik in fast jedem Auto steckt.

Wir suchen einen Projektmanager (m/w) für die Entwicklung eines computergestützten Warnsystems bei Gefahren im Straßenverkehr. Sie sind Leiter eines internationalen Teams von 25 Ingenieuren und IT-Spezialisten.

Sie haben ein abgeschlossenes Studium in Informatik und besitzen angemessene Berufserfahrung. Sie sind es gewohnt, selbstständig Ideen zu entwickeln und diese in die Praxis umzusetzen. Sie verstehen es, andere für Ihre Pläne zu begeistern und einzunehmen. Sie sprechen fließend Englisch, sodass Sie keine Schwierigkeiten haben, innerhalb des Unternehmens bzw. mit unseren globalen Partnern zu kommunizieren. Sie sind bereit, mehrere Monate im Jahr unterwegs zu sein, um vor Ort nach Lösungen zu suchen.

Falls wir Ihr Interesse geweckt haben, richten Sie Ihre Bewerbung bis zum 22. Mai an Herrn Müller, Personalabteilung IT Solutions, Postfach 1045, München.

Unit 3

Media words

1 Setze die passenden Begriffe in die Lücken ein.

advertising – commercials – digital – download – Internet – influence – mobile phones – printed – social networking sites – source – television – text messages

Surprisingly, teenagers today don't spend as much time as their parents in front of the ______________________. Instead, most teenagers prefer surfing the ______________________. They use it as a ______________________ of information and entertainment. But ______________________ have the greatest ______________________ on teenagers' lives these days. The ______________________ industry has reacted to the time spent online and has created Internet ______________________ especially for teenagers. Today, people have access to a lot of media using their ______________________: they can ______________________ music, exchange photos or videos and send ______________________ to their friends all at the same time. However, even in this ______________________ world there are still lots of people who read ______________________ media like magazines or newspapers.

Film words

2 Suche im Wortgitter die englischen Entsprechungen der deutschen Begriffe.

Anweisung – Dämmerlicht – Totale – heranfahren / heranzoomen – Nahaufnahme – Halbnahe – Hintergrundkommentar – Regisseur – Drehbuch – schneiden – Einstellung / Ansicht

M	F	O	R	M	V	A	A	D	D	E	R	T	U	V
O	I	V	O	N	I	U	M	Z	M	I	M	I	P	O
T	L	W	I	D	E	S	H	O	T	Z	U	I	O	U
H	M	E	T	H	W	B	M	O	S	D	F	R	E	A
V	S	A	P	P	E	L	R	M	E	R	N	L	R	T
O	C	H	S	O	F	T	L	I	G	H	T	I	N	G
I	R	E	R	H	J	L	B	N	N	F	E	G	A	I
C	I	M	A	U	S	D	G	J	K	M	F	H	E	R
E	P	T	M	E	D	I	U	M	S	H	O	T	O	M
O	T	E	W	A	S	R	R	T	R	Z	U	I	O	P
V	R	C	L	O	S	E	U	P	P	E	N	N	I	N
E	T	O	P	F	D	C	E	C	K	E	L	G	U	M
R	D	I	R	E	C	T	I	O	N	A	U	T	O	O
I	Z	R	E	N	B	O	R	T	U	N	H	D	F	R
C	U	T	R	U	N	R	T	Z	I	P	P	O	R	E

Word families

3 Setze Wörter aus der angegebenen Wortfamilie ein.

1. **excitement:** The show was so ____________________ that I forgot the time. You could feel the ____________________ of the audience. Everybody was very ____________________.
2. **to summarize:** I found the ____________________ plot of the book on the Internet. I can't ____________________ texts very well. I always get bad marks for my ____________________.

3. **surprise:** They ______________________ us with their visit last week. The ______________________ children stood there with their mouths open. This was a real ______________________.

4. **to write:** ______________________ more clearly, please. You risk bad marks in your ______________________ tests if the teacher can't read your hand ______________________.

5. **to speak:** The ______________________ was brilliant. He ______________________ without any accent. His ______________________ was very interesting.

Cause and effect

4 Ergänze die Lücken mit den angegebenen Begriffen.

so that – because – since – as a result – because of

I like the Internet ______________________ I love chatting with my friends on social networking sites. Some time ago my grandma also wanted to go online ______________________ she could keep in touch with the world. ______________________ my grandma spends more and more time in front of the computer, even more than I do. ______________________ that my grandpa started to write to her on Facebook when he wanted to tell her something. ______________________ she agrees that this is a stupid situation, they have decided to use the Internet less often.

False friends

5 Übersetze die Sätze ins Englische.

1. Der Kühlschrank ist fast leer.

___

2. Paul rannte, so schnell er konnte.

___

3. Meiner Meinung nach hast du recht.

___

4. Welche Bedeutung hat dieses Wort?

___

5. Wann bekomme ich mein Geld zurück?

___

6. Der Frauenmangel wird in China zum Problem.

___

Discussion phrases

6 Trage die Ausdrücke in die richtige Spalte der Tabelle ein.

I'm sure – you can't say that – I see that differently – I believe – I disagree – in my opinion – that's not true – it seems to me – I think you're wrong

Eigene Meinung	Widerspruch

Dynamic verbs and stative verbs

> Alle Zeitstufen im Englischen haben eine ***simple*-Form** und eine ***progressive*-Form**, z. B. *simple present* und *present progressive*.
>
> Verben, die eine **Tätigkeit** oder einen **Vorgang** beschreiben ***(dynamic verbs)***, können in der ***simple*- oder *progressive*-Form** stehen:
> I usually **work** hard for school.
> **I'm working** in the garden at the moment.
>
> Verben, die eine **Sinneswahrnehmung**, **Meinung**, einen **Wunsch** oder einen **Zustand** beschreiben (***stative verbs***), stehen in der Regel in der ***simple*-Form:**
> Stop it. That **sounds** awful. – I **think** this is my mobile.
> We **want** to go to Spain next summer.
> Jean **has been** very happy since she met Mike.
>
> Manchmal beschreiben die gleichen Verben auch eine **Tätigkeit**. Du kannst sie dann auch in der ***progressive*-Form** verwenden. Achte dabei aber auf Bedeutungsunterschiede:
> You **look** much better than last week. (Bedeutung: aussehen)
> What **are** you **looking** for? (Bedeutung: suchen)

7 Setze die Verben in Klammern in die richtige Form des *present tense* (*simple* oder *progressive*).

Sally: I ____like____ (like) rap. The lyrics ____are____ (be) very important for me.

Carol: Oh no, I ____think____ (think) rap music is too aggressive. I sometimes even ____feel____ (feel) frightened. I've just seen a hip-hop dance group on TV and now I'm ____planing____ (plan) to join one. I really ____love____ (love) hip-hop and I ____wishing____ (wish) I could dance like the stars in the music videos.

Jo: We _______________ (do) a school project on Mozart at the moment. I _______________ (know) it _______________ (sound) boring, but now I _______________ (want) to go to the opera.

Frank: I _______________ (prefer) rock music to any other kind of music. My dad _______________ (play) in a 1980s-style band. Look, I _______________ (wear) their band T-shirt.

8 Setze das Verb in Klammern in die *simple-* oder *progressive-*Form des *present tense*. Achte dabei auf die Bedeutungsunterschiede.

1. The tourists _______________ (be) in the coach.
2. Stop it! You _______________ (be) silly.
3. Charles _______________ (have) got a new mobile.
4. We _______________ (have) breakfast.
5. She _______________ (feel) her way to the door.
6. I _______________ (not feel) well today.

9 Max hat in seiner Mail an einen Freund in Nottingham einige Fehler bei den *simple-* und *progressive-*Formen gemacht. Finde die 15 Fehler und korrigiere sie.

Hi Steve
I've seen Leonie for three months now. I'm thinking she is my great love. We do a lot of things together. We were going to a concert last Friday and we enjoyed it very much. I brought her home after that. We were standing in front of her house and I held her close as it was being cold. Suddenly she gave me a kiss.
We're loving every minute of being together, and when we aren't being together, we are texting each other all the time. Some of my friends are believing that I'm being silly, but they don't understand. I'm feeling happy when we're together. On the other hand I don't mean to ignore them totally. I'm loving everything about Leonie. Her hair smells wonderful, she's wearing nice jeans and she looks just beautiful.
I think of asking her to go to the cinema next Saturday. There's a film we haven't been seeing yet. I hope she's having time because she's doing an important project at school at the moment.
Oh, my mobile rings. Maybe it's Leonie.
See you
Max

Emphasis: inversion

Um etwas zu betonen, kannst du im Englischen die **Inversion** benutzen. Dabei **weichst du von der üblichen Satzstellung** *subject – verb – object* ab. Du leitest den Satz mit einer negativen adverbialen Bestimmung ein und stellst ein Hilfsverb vor das Subjekt.
Not only does he use his mobile during lessons, but he also talks with his class mates.

10 Mache den Text lebendiger, indem du die Inversion benutzt, wo sie möglich ist.

One night my phone rang. I didn't think for a moment that this phone call would change my life forever. When I answered the phone a voice said, "It's Bill Gates speaking." I wouldn't have believed this in my wildest dreams, so I simply said, "Stop joking."
But the man went on to tell me he had heard of my work as a computer engineer and wanted to offer me a job.
I was having breakfast the next morning when I got an e-mail. I didn't think for one moment that this mail might have something to do with the phone call the night before. But Bill Gates made me the same offer again. I was not only surprised but also very excited. I would never have thought that such a dream could come true.
So I arranged a meeting at his office in America. I had hardly entered the building when Bill Gates greeted me in the entrance hall.
I've been working for him for two years now and I haven't regretted that decision for a minute. I have never had a more interesting time in my life.

Emphasis: emphatic do and it is / it was

Du kannst Sätze auch betonen oder Dinge richtigstellen, indem du eine Form von ***do*** vor den **Infinitiv** stellst *(emphatic do)*:
Why didn't you feed the dog? I **did** feed him.

Um etwas richtigzustellen, kannst du außerdem ***it is / it was*** verwenden. Der Rest des Satzes wird mit einem Relativsatz oder einem *that*-Satz angehängt:
It was dad who cleaned the kitchen (not my brother).

11 Übersetze die Satzteile und verwende dabei das *emphatic do.*

1. Good morning, Mrs Walker. (Nehmen Sie doch bitte Platz.)

___

2. Chris, you never put your dishes away after breakfast. – That's not true, mum! (Ich habe es heute Morgen wirklich weggeräumt.)

___

3. I can't understand what our tour guide is explaining. (Sei doch bitte leise.)

___

4. This was a perfect holiday. (Wir haben jede Minute genossen.)

___

12 Sally muss einiges richtigstellen, was ihre Großmutter falsch verstanden hat. Bilde Sätze mit *it is / it was.*

1. *Grandma:* Sally, you're going out with John, aren't you?

Sally: No, grandma, ___

___. (Jeff)

2. *Grandma:* Oh yes, Jeff. Didn't you meet him at Laura's party?

Sally: No, ___. (school concert)

3. *Grandma:* And now you're going to the cinema.

Sally: No, ____

____. (party)

4. *Grandma:* Oh, of course. But your sister is going out with John.

Sally: No, ____

____. (Jo)

Emphasis: self-pronouns and adverbs of degree

Mit den **Pronomen auf *-self/-selves*** betonst du, dass jemand etwas selbst getan hat:
I downloaded the software **myself**.

Auch mit **Gradadverbien** (*adverbs of degree*) kannst du etwas besonders hervorheben. Sie stehen vor dem Wort, das betont werden soll:
You **really play** too many computer games.

13 Trage die passenden Pronomen auf *-self/-selves* ein.

1. Carl repaired the computer ____________________.
2. Even my parents think that we need a faster Internet connection. They say so ____________________.
3. A computer system needs regular updates. That ____________________ is too difficult for many people.
4. We had a computer problem yesterday. But we found a solution ____________________.
5. She had written the computer programme ____________________.
6. I always download software ____________________.

14 Betone den unterstrichenen Satzteil mit einem passenden Gradadverb.

1. A strange film was made in the old castle.

___

2. One of the actors was an old man.

___

3. Making the film was difficult.

___

4. In the end, the film was well produced.

___

Emphasis with what

Du kannst auch einen vorangestellten ***what***-Satz benutzen, um etwas zu betonen.

Möchtest du das (direkte) **Objekt** betonen, so beginnst du den Hauptsatz mit einer Form von ***to be***:
What I like best about the cinema **are** the commercials.

Möchtest du dagegen das **Verb** besonders betonen, so benutzt du im *what*-Satz eine Form von ***to do*** und im zweiten Satzteil das **Verb als Infinitiv** mit oder ohne *to*:
What Trevor **did was** (to) take photos of the accident.

15 Bilde Sätze aus den Wörtern.

1. we all – are – what – holidays – need

___

2. told us – very interesting – was – Sarah – what

___

3. my dad – turn off – the computer – what – was – did

4. is – what – James – very dangerous – does

Simple present and present progressive

Mit dem ***simple present*** drückst du aus, dass eine Handlung **regelmäßig**, oder **gewohnheitsmäßig** ausgeführt wird. Du benutzt es auch bei allgemeingültigen Tatsachen oder dann, wenn Handlungsabläufe berichtet werden:
Steve **plays** football twice a week.
Pigs **don't fly**.
Harry Potter **lives** with his aunt and uncle, but later he **goes** to Hogwarts and **meets** lots of new friends.

Mit dem ***present progressive*** drückst du aus, dass eine Handlung **gerade stattfindet**, also noch nicht abgeschlossen ist:
I'm listening to a CD at the moment.
Are you **watching** this film?

Die Handlung, die im *present progressive* steht, kann sich auch über eine längere Zeit hinziehen:
Tarantino **is making** another film this year.

16 Entscheide, ob du *simple present* oder *present progressive* benutzen musst, und streiche die falsche Form durch.

1. I play / ~~am playing~~ in the school football team.
2. We ~~play~~ / are playing well this season.
3. Sue ~~does~~ / is doing her homework at the moment.
4. Luke does / ~~is doing~~ his homework regularly.
5. Listen, Jeff ~~plays~~ / is playing the trumpet again!
6. Sorry, nobody ~~works~~ / is working today.
7. My sister doesn't work / ~~isn't working~~ as a teacher.
8. The earth moves / ~~is moving~~ around the sun.

Present perfect and simple past

Mit dem ***present perfect*** drückst du eine Handlung aus, die zwar **abgeschlossen** ist, aber noch **Auswirkungen** auf die Gegenwart oder Zukunft hat:
I'**ve** already **done** my homework. Now I can call my friend.

Du benutzt es auch, um zu sagen, dass eine Handlung oder ein Ereignis **noch nicht eingetreten** ist:
Carol **hasn't finished** the exercise yet.

Mit dem ***simple past*** sprichst du dagegen über eine Handlung, die bereits **abgeschlossen** ist. Sie fand zu einem konkret bestimmbaren Zeitpunkt in der Vergangenheit statt. Das *simple past* ist außerdem die Erzählzeit für die Vergangenheit:
I **watched** a boring film yesterday.
Luke **got** up at 7 o'clock that morning. He **went** to the bathroom and **had** a shower. After that he **made** himself breakfast.

17 Setze die Verben in die richtige Form (*present perfect* oder *simple past*).

1. I ____________________ (buy) a very interesting book yesterday.
2. Jake ____________________ (spend) the last of his money. He can't buy a ticket for the bus.
3. The USA ____________________ (become) independent in 1776.
4. I ____________________ (see) this movie twice so far.
5. When ____________________ you ____________________ (come) home last night?
6. I ____________________ (speak) to Mr Taylor five minutes ago.
7. Megan ____________________ (not be) to Germany yet.
8. We ____________________ (eat) an awful pizza for lunch today.

Present perfect progressive

Mit dem ***present perfect progressive*** drückst du aus, dass eine Handlung in der Vergangenheit begonnen hat und ununterbrochen bis jetzt andauert, also noch nicht abgeschlossen ist. Im Gegensatz zum ***present perfect*** wird beim ***present perfect progressive*** die Dauer betont.
Häufig stehen in Sätzen mit dem *present perfect progressive* ***since*** (für die Angabe des Zeitpunkts) und ***for*** (für die Angabe des Zeitraums):
I've been watching this film **for** one hour now.
It's almost midnight. They **have been sitting** and **talking since** dinner.

18 Setze die Verben in das *present perfect progressive*. Ergänze außerdem *since* oder *for*.

1. Tracy and Jean ______________________ (play) the guitar __________ two hours.
2. Rob ______________________ (wait) for his girlfriend __________ twenty minutes.
3. They ______________________ (run) through the park __________ 9 o'clock this morning.
4. Dad ______________________ (read) the newspaper __________ he came home from work.
5. This shop ______________________ (sell) tea __________ more than 150 years.
6. Mr Clark ______________________ (ride) his bike to work __________ he crashed his car.

Past progressive

Mit dem ***past progressive*** drückst du aus, dass eine Handlung zu einem bestimmten Zeitpunkt in der Vergangenheit gerade ablief, also noch nicht abgeschlossen war:
I **was watching** the news on TV last night at eight o'clock.

Wenn diese länger andauernde Handlung durch eine neue, plötzlich einsetzende Handlung unterbrochen wird, steht diese neue Handlung im *simple past*:
Ruby **was doing** her homework when her mobile **rang**.

19 Inspector Whodunit untersucht den Mord am reichen Mr Neverenoughmoney. Vervollständige die Aussagen der Haushaltsmitglieder. Benutze das *past progressive*.

Whodunit: What were you doing this morning between 9 and 10 o'clock?

Old Mrs Greedy: I ______________________ (check) on the maids *(Hausmädchen)*. They are always lazy.

The maids: We ______________________ (clean) the rooms downstairs.

Tina and Tony: We ______________________ (play) in our room. But we saw our grandma when she ______________________ (walk) along the corridor.

Mr Green: I ______________________ (cut) down the old tree. I saw Mrs Greedy. She ______________________ (talk) very loudly to Mr Neverenoughmoney.

Mr Nolimit: I ______________________ (repair) the old Bentley in the garage when I heard the shot.

20 Vervollständige die Sätze, indem du das Verb ins *present perfect* oder *past tense* setzt (jeweils *simple* oder *progressive*).

1. On the day of the Hardys' move, it ____________________ (start) to rain while they ____________________ (carry) their furniture to the street in front of their house.
2. But the big lorry which they ____________________ (need) ____________________ (not be) there.
3. Everything ____________________ (get) wet while they ____________________ (wait).
4. When the lorry finally ____________________ (arrive) they first ____________________ (put) the sofa inside.
5. While they ____________________ (still carry) their furniture outside, the lorry driver suddenly ____________________ (drive) away with most of their things.
6. Since then the Hardys ____________________ (live) without most of their furniture.
7. The police ____________________ (try) to find the driver but they ____________________ (not be) successful yet.
8. As the insurance company *(Versicherung)* ____________________ (not pay) any money yet, the Hardys ____________________ (get used) to living without a sofa and chairs.

Past perfect (progressive)

Mit dem ***past perfect*** kannst du ausdrücken, dass eine Handlung noch vor einer anderen Handlung in der Vergangenheit stattfand (Vorvergangenheit). Deshalb steht das ***past perfect*** oft in Verbindung mit dem *simple past*:
I **had turned** off all the lights before I went to bed.

Auch das ***past perfect*** hat eine *progressive*-Form. Das ***past perfect progressive*** drückt eine Handlung aus, die gerade ablief, als eine andere Handlung einsetzte:
We **had been waiting** for half an hour when the bus finally came.

21 Setze die Verben ins *simple past* oder ins *(simple) past perfect.*

My grandfather ____________ (be) born in a small village in Jamaica in 1929. He ____________ (leave) school when he ____________ (be) 14 years old. He ____________ (already work) in a few different jobs when he ____________ (decide) to go to Britain. He ____________ (save) some money, so he ____________ (buy) a ticket for a ship to England. When he ____________ (arrive) in London he ____________ (realize) that someone ____________ (steal) most of his money. He ____________ (get) a job as a dishwasher in a restaurant, but he only ____________ (stay) there for a few months. However, he ____________ (not like) his second job at the London harbour any better. This ____________ (not be) what he ____________ (leave) Jamaica for.

But in his new job he ____________________ (meet) a lot of other immigrants from the Caribbean. None of them ____________________ (like) the food in England. They ____________________ (miss) their traditional food. My grandpa ____________________ (remember) that his mother ____________________ (teach) him a lot of recipes. So he ____________________ (open) one of the first Caribbean restaurants in London.

22 Ergänze die Sätze mit dem *past perfect progressive.*

1. Jeff was angry because the film had already started. He ______________________________ (wait) for his girlfriend for more than half an hour.
2. In the evening Becky and Jenny didn't have any money left. They ______________________________ (shop) the whole afternoon.
3. Kelly was glad that school was over. She ______________________________ (think) about her boyfriend all day.
4. Mr Brown's arms hurt when he went to bed. He ______________________________ (paint) the kitchen for five hours.
5. At dinner Ruth felt tired. She ______________________________ (study) for her exams since lunchtime.

Mixed bag: tenses

23 Setze die Verben in die richtige Zeit.

TV ______________________ (become) popular in the 1950s. In Britain, for example, a lot of people ______________________ (buy) their first TV sets to watch how Elizabeth ______________________ (become) queen in 1953. As the importance of television ______________________ (grow), more and more programmes ______________________ (appear). Suddenly people ______________________ (can) watch the news. Before, they ______________________ (just listen) to them on the radio or ______________________ (read) the newspapers. Since the 1960s more and more entertainment programmes such as soap operas ______________________ (appear) on television. At first they ______________________ (show) a world in which everybody ______________________ (live) a happy life, so that people ______________________ (can dream) while they ______________________ (watch) the programme. But after some time the soaps ______________________ (start) to show more realistic situations. “East Enders”, which ______________________ (be) one of the most important British soap operas today, ______________________ (be) set in London’s East End and ______________________ (show) all the problems of the people who ______________________ (live) there. This trend ______________________ (continue) in the new millennium and recently reality shows ______________________ (become) a big success. Almost every channel ______________________ (produce) its own reality show. As these programmes ______________________ (be) often interrupted by commercials, they ______________________ (be) a big market for the advertising industry too. So viewers who ______________________ (watch) the shows ______________________ (not always enjoy) them.

24 Übersetze ins Englische. Achte dabei auf die Zeit.

1. Ich habe gestern meinen Englischlehrer in der Stadt gesehen.

____

2. Wir wohnen seit zehn Jahren in diesem Haus.

____

3. Nachdem ich ein neues Handy gekauft hatte, verkaufte ich mein altes.

____

4. Josh ging gerade die Straße entlang, als ihm ein Reporter ein paar Fragen stellte.

____

5. Die Jacksons sind einkaufen gegangen. Es ist niemand zu Hause.

____

Reading: Cyberbullying

While cyberbullying or Internet bullying doesn't affect a large number of kids, for those who are affected, life can turn into hell. This new type of bullying can have even more serious effects than "normal" bullying. Victims of cyberbullying don't have a safe refuge. When bullying happens at school or work, its victims are left alone at weekends and in the evenings. But attacks via the Internet or text messages can reach you anytime, anywhere, even at home. Once a picture, a video or a piece of gossip is online, it quickly moves through the virtual world. It can be very difficult or even impossible to have it removed.

The culprits can hide behind fake names. This makes it easy for them to be ruder and more aggressive than they would ever be off the Internet, as no one will ever know who is behind these humiliations. So it could be that cyberbullies are even younger or physically weaker than the kids they attack. However, there seems to be at least one positive aspect: during school holidays fewer cases of cyberbullying are reported. This would suggest that the culprits often belong to the school community and might therefore be identified. Unfortunately, for many victims this makes little or no difference. When cyberbullying has reached a point where victims can't deal with it anymore, many feel that their only way out is to leave school, or worse, commit suicide.

So what can be done against cyberbullying? First of all, it is important for kids as well as for adults to realize that they must be careful what they share on the Internet. What some teenagers might think of as a cool video or photo of themselves could start a storm of nasty comments, or it might be manipulated with the help of modern technology. What ends up being looked at or watched by thousands of people might be something altogether different from the original.

Parents play an important role in that they can show their kids how to use the Internet safely. It's useless to tell kids not to visit certain websites: many will do it anyway – secretly, if necessary. Instead, parents should show an interest in the sites their kids are visiting. But if they want to teach their kids what it means to be careful Internet users, they must above all behave carefully themselves. This means that they will have to think twice before sharing family pictures or stories about their personal lives on the Internet. Another important point for parents is not to blame their kids when they have become victims of cyberbullying. After all, in most cases they haven't done anything wrong. Instead, parents should support their kids in every possible way to end the attacks.

25 Ordne den unbekannten Wörtern aus dem Text die passende Definition zu.

victim	a person who has done something wrong
refuge	to say or think that somebody has done something wrong
to remove	an act which makes somebody feel a sense of shame
culprit	somebody who has been / is attacked
humiliation	to get rid of something
to commit suicide	to kill oneself
to manipulate	to change something, to make somebody act the way you want
to blame	safe place which offers protection from somebody or something

26 Entscheide, ob die Aussagen wahr *(true)* oder falsch *(false)* sind.

1. At home victims are safe from cyberbullying.

☐ true ☐ false

2. The culprits can be found easily.

☐ true ☐ false

3. The culprit often knows the victim.

☐ true ☐ false

4. Kids have dropped out of school because of cyberbullying.

☐ true ☐ false

5. There is no need for parents to be careful with the Internet.

☐ true ☐ false

6. Parents must tell their kids which sites they can visit.

☐ true ☐ false

Reading for research: Teenage media habits

The young generation today is confronted by an unprecedented choice of media. There are still the old newspapers, magazines and books, but printed media are gradually being replaced by electronic media, like mobile phones, tablets and of course the Internet. So how is the teenage generation being influenced by modern electronic media?

First of all, there is hardly a teenager today who hasn't got a mobile. Much to the surprise of their parents or grandparents, the mobile phone isn't much used as a phone. Instead of talking to other people, teenagers prefer to send text messages with their mobiles. The average amount of text messages sent by teenagers is double that of the second most active age group, young adults.

For someone from the older generations it might be a strange or even funny scene to see a couple of teenagers sitting next to each other and silently hacking away on their mobiles without talking to each other. But teenagers not only exchange messages in what to people not familiar with the language teenagers use seems like a secret code, but they also exchange photos or videos, either made by the teenagers themselves or downloaded from the Internet.

Teenagers are very active users of mobile phones and the Internet, the advertising industry is making the most of this. It creates and places ads specially produced for teenagers on those sites most popular within that age group. Teenagers spend a lot of time online, but mostly visit social networking sites. They usually register on those sites as soon as they are allowed to. Peer pressure seems to play an important role here: when all your friends and classmates have already registered and put their personal profiles online, you don't want to be left out!

Although old media are being replaced step by step by new electronic media, there is still one item that seems to stand firm: television. Teenagers still spend a lot of time in front of it, but, maybe surprisingly, their parents might spend even more time watching TV. But on the other hand, this time difference is again used by the teenagers texting on their mobiles or sitting in front of the computer chatting or playing games.

27 Für ein Referat zum Thema „British teens and media“ bist du auf diesen Beitrag im Internet gestoßen. Überfliege den Text *(skim)* und überlege, ob er für dein Referat brauchbar ist. Notiere die Gründe für deine Entscheidung.

Der Text ist ☐ brauchbar. ☐ nicht brauchbar.

Gründe: ______________________________

28 Finde heraus, wie britische Teenager ihr Handy verwenden (*scan*) und notiere die Stichpunkte auf Englisch.

Listening: Going to the cinema 8

29 Wer möchte welche Art von Film sehen und warum?

Dialogue 1

Boy: kind of film: ______________________________

Reasons: ______________________________

____

Girl: kind of film: ______________________________

Reasons: ______________________________

____

Dialogue 2

Girl: kind of film: ______________________________

Reasons: ______________________________

____

Boy: kind of film: ______________________________

Reasons: ______________________________

____

Dialogue 3

Boy: kind of film: ______________________________

Reasons: ______________________________

____

Girl: kind of film: ______________________________

Reasons: ______________________________

Listening: Media today – a discussion 9

30 Schreibe die Argumente, die für bzw. gegen die Nutzung des Internets genannt werden, in die Tabelle.

Pro	Con

Mediation: An interview with a pop star

31 Deine Austauschpartnerin aus England findet in einer Zeitschrift ein Interview mit einer ihrer Lieblingssängerinnen, Fiona Harris, und hat einige Fragen. Lies das Interview und hilf ihr beim Verständnis.

Fiona, Sie sind ständig unterwegs. Was vermissen Sie besonders?
Fiona: Ich versuche, so oft wie möglich zu Hause zu sein, aber wenn ich unterwegs bin, vermisse ich eine ganz bestimmte Art von Keksen, die ein Bäcker bei mir um die Ecke macht. Außerdem vermisse ich meine Lieblingssoap, aber die kann ich mittlerweile auch im Internet sehen.

Sie sehen immer fabelhaft aus. Können Sie uns Ihr Beauty-Geheimnis verraten?
Fiona: Öl! Ich benutze alle möglichen Öle für Körper und Haare; besonders aber Olivenöl und Kokosöl.

Ihr Vater stammt aus Schottland und Ihre Mutter aus Brasilien, aufgewachsen sind Sie aber in London. Welche Kultur hat Sie am meisten beeinflusst?
Fiona: Ich glaube, ich habe von jeder Kultur etwas abbekommen. Mir gefällt die Wärme und Herzlichkeit der Schotten, und ich besuche gerne meine Verwandten dort. Von meiner Mutter habe ich das Temperament, das Gefühl für Musik und Rhythmus mitbekommen, obwohl ich leider fast kein Portugiesisch spreche.

Wo wollen Sie dieses Jahr Ihren Urlaub verbringen?
Fiona: Ich habe schon viele wahnsinnig tolle Gegenden und Orte gesehen, aber ob Sie es glauben oder nicht, ich werde diesmal für ein paar Tage in den Schwarzwald fahren. Die Natur dort ist einfach sagenhaft.

Sie gelten auch als eine Stilikone. Was ist Ihr Lieblingstrend für nächsten Sommer?
Fiona: Ich liebe knallige Farben und leichte Stoffe. Für mich ist es aber wichtig, dass ich mich wohl fühle in meinen Klamotten.

Wie sieht das Leben der Fiona Harris in fünf oder zehn Jahren aus?
Fiona: Oje, darüber habe ich mir ehrlich gesagt noch keine großen Gedanken gemacht. Vielleicht stehe ich noch immer auf der Bühne; vielleicht kümmere ich mich um ein oder zwei Kinder, wer weiß.

Vielen Dank für das Interview.

1. Oh, I love her style and her appearance. Her skin looks so soft. How does she do it?

2. What will be her look for the summer?

3. And what about her holidays? Where is she going to spend them?

4. Uh! Why is that?

5. Will there be a new CD soon?

Writing in an Internet forum

32 In einem Internetforum äußern sich Teenager darüber, ob Handys an Schulen erlaubt sein sollen. Schreibe einen eigenen Beitrag.

Hi everybody
I use my mobile as often as all my friends. But there should be a time without mobiles: at school. Some of my classmates are busier with their mobiles than with their exercises during lessons. I can't concentrate when they suddenly start laughing about some funny text message or video.
Ben (14) Leeds

Hi guys
Our generation can't live without mobiles; and that's a good thing. Mobiles are a great advantage in all situations, even at school.
Sometimes it's that there is something important you have to know (your dad can't pick you up after school, you have to meet somebody) or you missed something important in the lesson before and now you have to ask your friend. Mobiles can be used to get information, too. So why shouldn't they be allowed at school?
Janice (14) Bristol

Hi there
Last week, a teacher took away my mobile just because I was writing a short text message to my mum in the break. I think that's unfair. I didn't distract anyone and nobody had complained about me.
Our school rules say that we aren't allowed to use mobiles at school, but do they really have to be so strict?
Sophie (15) Stuttgart

Revision B

Reading: How to deal with money

Almost every teenager these days has got a mobile phone or even a smartphone, but some of them find it difficult to pay the bills for their electronic equipment. It is therefore important that young people learn how to handle money from an early age.

The learning process will usually start as early as primary school. There are different opinions about which age children should be when they get their first pocket money; and of course how much they should get. It is important, however, that the pocket money is paid on a regular basis, usually on a certain day of the week, and that it is not too much. Thus children learn that money doesn't simply appear whenever they want it, but that they must manage with a limited sum.

So from an early age children find out what they can do with their money – and what they can't. Some will spend it on sweets, small toys or books. Others will put a part of their pocket money aside and save it. When they are older and start getting larger sums from relatives for Christmas or for their birthday, they might even take their money to a bank.

Pocket money should be increased step by step as the children grow older. Many of them will start to work in order to earn additional money. The age at which children are allowed to hold regular paid jobs is regulated by laws. Many teenagers start by taking the neighbour's dog for a walk once or twice a week or they do the shopping for the old lady next door.

Such jobs are called inofficial jobs: work that is normally done within house and family. When young people are employed for official jobs, the situation becomes more complicated. Teenagers helping in the local supermarket on Saturdays or doing a paper round once a week have to be of a certain age. There is also a limit to the number of hours per week young people are allowed to work.

However, by the time they hold jobs, young people should have been given responsibility for their own money. They will have learned by then that they have to pay for certain things themselves, e.g. DVDs, going to the cinema or downloading music. Many of them will start saving for bigger things: their own car or a holiday without their parents. Those who haven't learned how to handle money will find it very difficult to manage it wisely now.

Parents should show their children how to deal with money in everyday life and explain to them that they should be careful not to spend more money than they have. This means that on the one hand, parents should give their children the freedom to handle their own money. On the other hand, adults should keep an eye on their children's financial situation.

Unfortunately, mobile phones are often a source of financial problems among young people. So parents should help their children to find a mobile phone with a suitable contract. For when it comes to signing a contract the parent or parents take full responsibility for the payment of the bill if their child is younger than 18. Adults should also make sure that teenagers know about the hidden costs: that there are special (and expensive) services, that each text message costs money or that there can be problems when surfing the internet. It is often a good idea to arrange a certain limit for the mobile bill (a prepaid service is useful).

1 Vervollständige die Sätze mit den Informationen aus dem Text.

1. Most young people use electronic ______________________ today.
2. There is no definite ______________________ about how much pocket money should be given.
3. There are ______________________ that regulate when young people can get an official job.
4. ______________________ should set a good example in financial issues.
5. The biggest financial ______________________ for young people today is their mobile phone bill.

Listening: A guided tour through a film studio 10

2 Höre dir die Führung durch das Filmstudio an und unterstreiche jeweils die richtige Aussage.

1. The tour guide can / cannot show all areas of the studio.
2. There are / aren't people on the staff who don't have anything to do with film making.
3. It is possible / is not possible to get a role as an extra.
4. Visitors are / aren't allowed to use their mobiles during the tour.
5. The films are / aren't kept secret.
6. Computers are / aren't used for the production of commercials.
7. The visitor centre offers / doesn't offer a lot of things.

Writing for a blog

3 Versetze dich in die Rolle eines der Filmstudio-Besucher und schreibe darüber einen Gastbeitrag für das Blog eines englischen Freundes.

Mediation: Understanding copyright

4 Ihr wollt ein Schulprojekt ins Netz stellen und möchtet wissen, welche Bilder, Filme und Tondokumente ihr dafür verwenden dürft. Erkläre deinen Mitschülern und Mitschülerinnen kurz auf Deutsch die Rechtslage.

You can put pictures or other images online if you are their creator. If you aren't, you have to ask the creator or artist first. You are not allowed to simply scan and use pictures, images, cartoons or similar illustrations from newspapers, magazines, calendars, books or other printed or digital material.
The same is of course true for photographs. You must not put a photograph online if the person who took it hasn't allowed it. But even if you took the photograph yourself, you must be careful. It is essential that the persons shown in your picture say that you may publish it. (However, the rule is less strict when the people in the photograph are not as important as other things, e. g. buildings.)

You may not put individual pictures or sequences from films or television programmes online, as the film or the programme is protected as a whole. Most of the big entertainment companies, which own the rights for popular characters and cartoons, have very strict copyright rules, and it can be very expensive to break them.

The same is also true if you want to put songs or sound files online. On the other hand there is no problem if you have recorded the sound file yourself, unless sounds produced by someone else can be heard. But all that does not mean that it is absolutely impossible to put material online which has been created by someone else. On the Internet you can find lots of free-to-use photos and images. But always carefully check the source of the material you want to use for copyright information.

Unit 4

Talking about human rights

1 Ergänze die Lücken mit den Übersetzungen der Begriffe in Klammern.

1. child labour *(Kinderarbeit)* is still ____________ *(geduldet)* in some developing world *(Entwicklungsländern)*.
2. A ____________ *(Diktator)* can't rule without a ____________ *(Geheimpolizei)*.
3. ____________ *(trotz)* ____________ *(Chancengleichheit)*, the situation of women is not ____________ *(zufriedenstellend)*.
4. The ____________ *(Würde)* of ____________ *(Lesben)* and ____________ *(Schwule)* is often not respected.
5. ____________ *(Mut / Tapferkeit)* was the only ____________ *(angemessene)* way to end ____________ *(Rassentrennung)*.
6. The ____________ *(Vorstellung / Konzept)* of ____________ *(Sklaverei)* was ____________ *(üblich / verbreitet)* in all societies of the ____________ *(antik)* world.

7. The ________________ *(Parlament)* ________________ *(verabschiedete)* the ________________ *(nötige)* ________________ *(Gesetz)* against ________________ *(alltäglichen)* ________________ *(Rassismus)*.

8. Your ________________________ *(Doppelmoral)* are ________________ (*unausstehlich*) and you ________________ *(beleidigen / verletzen)* other people.

Opposites

2 Finde jeweils das Gegenteil der Begriffe und trage es ein.

Down:
1. fact
2. integration
3. fearless
8. freedom
9. female
10. life
12. noisy

Across:
4. aggressive
5. special
6. modern
7. dissonant
11. thin
13. most
14. public
15. eastern

Synonyms

3 Ergänze die Synonyme der Begriffe in Klammern.

1. I ____________________ (got) a nice letter yesterday.
2. It took very long to pass this ____________________ (law).
3. If you don't study, you won't get good ____________________ (grades).
4. Rose was ____________________ (very frightened) when she heard the news.
5. The politician was ____________________ (killed) in bright daylight.
6. Traffic is a ____________________ (everyday) problem in most big cities.
7. This ring is of great ____________________ (value) to me.
8. I can't ____________________ (deal with) his strange ideas.

Collocations

4 Unterstreiche jeweils die zwei Substantive, die zum Verb passen.

1. to free:
animals – slaves – democracy – relationships

2. to recruit:
an observer – a soldier – a concept – an activist

3. to spread:
butter – a mob – a carpet – a rumor

4. to vote for:
a woman – an ingredient – a song – death

5. to receive:
a present – a target – a postcard – a solution

6. to pass:
lyrics – segregation – a law – the station

5 Welches Adjektiv passt zu welchem Substantiv? Verwende die Kombination in jeweils einem Satz.

Adjectives: authoritarian – curious – exotic – peaceful – realistic
Nouns: activist – child – concept – ingredient – regime

1. ______________________________
2. ______________________________
3. ______________________________
4. ______________________________
5. ______________________________

Prepositions

6 Ergänze jeweils die passende Präposition.

1. Our team qualified __________ the next round.
2. Tracy has spread nasty rumors __________ her last boyfriend.
3. I can't identify __________ the characters in that book.
4. My mum complained __________ the service in the hotel.
5. My grandfather always spoke __________ against racism.
6. I don't know who to vote __________.
7. You can't judge people __________ their clothes.
8. My dad has always been a role model __________ me.
9. There are a lot of references __________ politics in this song.

Word families

7 Ergänze die verwandten Wörter in der Tabelle. Benutze dann die Begriffe aus der Tabelle, um sie in die Lücken des Textes zu setzen.

Verb	Noun	Adjective
tolerate		
		free
	respect	
die		

1. We need more ______________________ in our society.
2. We should ______________________ other cultures more.
3. The fight for ______________________ has always been an important issue.
4. Only ______________________ people can live together peacefully.
5. A ______________________ way of living together is very important.
6. Only if we show ______________________ to others can we expect the same from them.
7. People who ______________________ while fighting for a religious cause have a very special status in some societies.
8. For them ______________________ doesn't mean the end.

Tipp

Du kannst auch Partizipien als Adjektive verwenden. Beachte dabei:
Das *past participle* hat passive Bedeutung.
Das *present participle* hat aktive Bedeutung.

Adjectives

8 Entscheide, ob das Adjektiv als Substantiv verwendet wird oder nicht, und setze die notwendigen Artikel ein.

1. ________________ (rich) often live in separated areas.

2. There are a lot of ________________ (rich) people in this club.

3. A lot of ________________ (old) people live alone.

4. ________________ (old) might become a problem for younger generations.

5. A ________________ (poor) man is begging for money.

6. The government doesn't do enough for ________________ (poor).

9 *Characterization:* Entscheide, ob die Adjektive positive, neutrale oder negative Eigenschaften ausdrücken, und sortiere sie in die Tabelle.

aggressive – amazing – angry – ambitious – attractive – authoritarian – average – awesome – awful – bald – beautiful – boring brave – clever – cold – confident

Positive	Neutral	Negative
________________	________________	________________
________________	________________	________________
________________	________________	________________
________________	________________	________________
________________	________________	________________
________________	________________	________________
________________	________________	________________

The gerund

Das *gerund* ist die ***ing*-Form** des Verbs, die wie ein **Nomen** verwendet wird. Im Satz kann es die Funktion des **Subjekts** oder des **Objekts** haben:
Reading books is great. (Subjekt)
I love **reading** books. (Objekt)

Häufig findest du das *gerund* nach Wendungen aus
- **Adjektiv + Präposition:** He is **good at telling** jokes.
- **Verb + Präposition:** I **look forward to going** on holidays.
- **Substantiv + Präposition:** We had **the chance of meeting** the president.

10 Amy stellt sich ihrer neuen Klasse vor. Setze die Verben ins *gerund*.

Hi everybody. My name is Amy Donald. I love reading (read). I'm a big fan of Harry Potter. I love watching (watch) the films too, and I'm dreaming of visiting (visit) the places where the films were made. I also enjoy riding (ride) my bike. Actually, I prefer riding (ride) the bike to walking (walk) and I also don't like taking (take) the bus because I hate standing (stand) in a crowded bus.
I enjoy spending (spend) time with my friends. I love meeting (meet) people and makeing (make) new friends. I play two instruments, but I prefer playing (play) the guitar to practicing (practice) the piano.
Now I hope you don't mind me talking (talk) so much. I'm looking forward to getting (get) to know you all.

11 Stammtischparolen. Setze die passende Präposition ein und bilde das *gerund* aus den Verben in Klammern.

to – for – on – at – in

1. This government is really bad ______________ (rule) the country.
2. Those politicians are only famous ______________ (raise) taxes *(Steuern)*.
3. They are just keen ______________ (stay) in power.
4. They are not interested ______________ (listen to) the people.
5. We have got used ______________ (live) with useless politicians.

12 Übersetze die Sätze ins Englische. Verwende dabei *gerunds*.

1. Die Aktivisten hatten Gelegenheit, die Ausbeuterfirma zu besuchen.

____

____

2. Sie waren wütend darüber, Kinder bei der Arbeit zu sehen.

____

____

3. Die Arbeiter hatten Angst, mit den Aktivisten zu reden.

____

____

4. Aber die Aktivisten hatten Übung darin, solche Leute zu befragen.

____

____

Preposition and gerund as adverbial

Auf bestimmte **Präpositionen** kann ein *gerund* folgen. Zusammen bilden Präposition und *gerund* eine **adverbiale Bestimmung** *(adverbial)*. Die häufigsten Präpositionen in diesem Zusammenhang sind *apart from, by, in spite of, instead of* und *without*.

13 Lies dir noch einmal den Text über Mahatma Gandhi auf Seite 8 durch, verbinde die Sätze und benutze dabei das *gerund* des Verbs in Klammern.

1. When Gandhi lived in South Africa, he worked as a lawyer **in spite of**	A. ________________ (fight) with weapons he chose non-violent forms of protest.
2. He fought for the rights of Indians in South Africa **without**	B. ________________ (be) considered the hero of Indian independence.
3. But then he moved to India **instead of**	C. ________________ (be) sent to prison a few times.
4. In India he informed himself of the people's problems **by**	D. ________________ (protest) against the discrimination against black South Africans, too.
5. He thought of new ways to protest **apart from**	E. (not be) white.
6. But **instead of**	F. ________________ (stay) in South Africa.
7. He continued his actions **in spite of**	G. ________________ (join) his actions.
8. More and more people supported him **by**	H. ________________ (continue) the fight.
9. Finally the British gave India its independence **instead of**	I. ________________ (travel) through the country.
10. But in the end, Gandhi was killed **in spite of**	J. just ________________ (write) letters to politicians.

The infinitive with to after for + (pro)noun

Nach *it is / it was* oder *there is / there are* + Adjektiv / Nomen + *for* + (Pro-)Nomen steht häufig der Infinitiv mit *to*:
It was difficult for the prime minister **to apologize**.

14 Bringe die Wörter in die richtige Reihenfolge und bilde einen sinnvollen Satz.

1. other opinions – for – to accept – it is – everybody – important

____

2. not always easy – parents – it is – to listen to – their teenage children – for

____

3. for – there are – strict rules – to follow – the media

____

4. hard – it is – to say – sometimes – the truth – politicians – for

____

5. shops – it is – for – to sell – wrong – dangerous toys

____

6. with equal job opportunities – laws – for employers – to provide – women – there are

____

7. for – the people – dangerous – not to listen to – it is – governments

____

The infinitive with and without to

Der Infinitiv **mit *to*** steht außerdem unter anderem
- nach **bestimmten Verben**, auch wenn ein **Objekt** zwischen Verb und *to* + Infinitiv steht:
  The **teacher wants me to sit** over there.
- nach **Superlativen, *the first / the last / the only one(s)***:
  He was **the youngest student to start** university that year.
- nach **Fragewörtern**:
  I didn't know who(m) to ask.

Der Infinitiv steht **ohne *to***:
- nach **modalen Hilfsverben**:
  I **must go now.**
- nach ***let*** und ***make***:
  The teacher **lets** me **sit** here.
- nach **Verben der Sinneswahrnehmung** *(verbs of perception)* + **direktem Objekt**, wenn die gesamte Handlung von Anfang bis Ende wahrgenommen wird:
  I **saw the man cross** the street.

15 Tony ist zum ersten Mal auf einer Demonstration und hat viele Fragen. Wandle sie in Sätze mit Fragewort und Infinitiv um.

1. How do I carry the sign?

   I don't know ______________________________ the sign.

2. What do I say if a reporter asks me questions?

   I have no idea ______________________________ if a reporter asks me questions.

3. Where do I go after the demonstration?

   I don't know ______________________________ after the demonstration.

4. Who do I ask if there is a problem?

   I don't know ______________________________ if there is a problem.

16 Setze *to* in die Lücken, wenn es nötig ist.

Hi, I'm Peggy. I want _to_ leave school as soon as possible, but my parents won't let me ______ do it. They expect me ______ go to university. But I would prefer ______ do on-the-job training, perhaps as a car mechanic. I would like ______ join an organisation which helps in developing countries so that I could ______ help the people there.

But it seems ______ be difficult for my parents ______ accept my plan. They don't want me ______ leave school. They say that if I really wish ______ help other people, I should also ______ finish school first. Then I would ______ have the chance ______ study. And after that, it might ______ be easier for me ______ decide what ______ do. It is their dream ______ see their daughter at university. I would be the first in our family ______ study.

17 Dieser Nachbar bekommt alles mit. Verbinde die Sätze mit einem Infinitiv nach dem *verb of perception*.

1. A police car sped up the road. I heard it.

____

2. Those kids played football on the fresh grass. I saw it.

____

3. My feet got wet in the rain. I felt it.

____

Gerund or infinitive?

Nach einigen Verben steht in der Regel ein ***gerund***. Dazu gehören: *to enjoy, to finish, to imagine, to talk about, to think of.*

Nach den meisten Verben kann entweder ein ***gerund*** oder ein **Infinitiv** stehen, ohne dass es einen Bedeutungsunterschied gibt.

Bei einigen Verben **unterscheidet** sich aber die **Bedeutung**, je nachdem, ob danach ein *gerund* oder der Infinitiv folgt, z. B.:
- *to mean* (*gerund*: bedeuten / Infinitiv: beabsichtigen, etwas zu tun),
- *to stop* (*gerund*: anhalten, um etwas zu tun / Infinitiv: aufhören, etwas zu tun),
- *to remember* (*gerund*: sich an etwas Vergangenes erinnern / daran denken, etwas zu tun),
- *to forget* (*gerund*: etwas Vergangenes vergessen / vergessen, etwas zu tun).

18 Ein ehemaliger Sklave erzählt. Entscheide, ob du die Verben in Klammern als *gerund* oder als Infinitiv mit oder ohne *to* benutzen musst.

I'll always remember __________________ (live) as a slave all those years ago. We started __________________ (work) very early. We weren't allowed to stop __________________ (have) a short break on very hot days. Sometimes it felt like __________________ (be) in hell. But we had to continue __________________ (collect) cotton *(Baumwolle)* till we had our lunch break. We were looking forward to __________________ (hear) the command to stop __________________ (work). Then we began __________________ (walk) to our small houses. At night, we often dreamed about __________________ (run) away. I'll never forget __________________ (see) the soldiers of the North, who were fighting for our liberty. It meant __________________ (be) free at last.

Modal auxiliaries and their substitutes

Die meisten **modalen Hilfsverben** kannst du nur im *present tense* verwenden (Ausnahme: *could*). Für alle anderen Zeiten benötigst du **Ersatzformen**.
Die häufigsten modalen Hilfsverben und ihre Ersatzformen sind:
- *can, can't: (not) able to / (not) allowed to*
- *must: have to*
- *mustn't, may not: not be allowed to*
- *needn't: not have to*
- *may: be allowed to*

19 Erkläre einem ausländischen Touristen die Bedeutung der Schilder. Verwende modale Hilfsverben oder ihre Ersatzformen.

①

②

③

④

⑤

⑥

⑦

⑧

1. ______________________________

2. ______________________________

3. ______________________________

4. ______________________________

5. ______________________________

6. ______________________________

7. ______________________________

8. ______________________________

Reported speech

Wenn du **direkte** in **indirekte Rede *(reported speech)*** umformst, musst du einige Regeln beachten:
- Achte auf notwendige Veränderungen **bei Pronomen, Zeit- und Ortsangaben**, die durch die veränderte Sprechersituation entstehen: *I → he / she; here → there; today → yesterday*
- Du musst das Verb um eine **Zeit in die Vergangenheit** verschieben ***(backshift)***, wenn das einleitende Verb im *past tense* steht.
- Achte bei **Fragen** auf die **Änderung des Satzbaus**: "Where is the station?" → He asked me where the station was.
- Indirekte Entscheidungsfragen werden mit *if* oder *whether* eingeleitet.
- **Aufforderungen** und **Befehle** werden mit einer **Infinitivkonstruktion** wiedergegeben: "Please be quiet." → They told us to be quiet.

20 Chris fragt seine Freunde, ob sie bei einem Benefizlauf mitmachen. Am nächsten Morgen berichtet er seinen Eltern.

1. John: "I am going to help my father paint our kitchen."

____

____

2. Megan: "I went to bed late yesterday so I am too tired to run the race."

____

____

3. Terry: "I won't have time because my cousin is coming."

____

____

4. Dan: "I'm sorry, but a friend has invited me to his house."

____

____

21 Am Abend erzählt Jack, was er an seinem ersten Tag in der neuen Schule erlebt hat.

1. Secretary: "Wait outside please."

___

2. Head teacher: "Find your classroom on your own."

___

3. Classmate: "Don't sit here. Sit next to Amy."

___

4. Teacher: "Don't leave your books on your desk, put them into your locker."

___

___

22 Setze die Fragen an den Premierminister in die indirekte Rede.

1. Reporter: "Have you already met the Queen?"

___

___

2. Reporter: "What will the future bring for our country?"

___

___

3. Reporter: "Why didn't you speak out against racism?"

___

___

4. Reporter: “When are you going to fly to Germany?”

---

5. Reporter: “Do you believe that Scotland will become independent?”

---

23 Becky möchte zu einer Demonstration zur Rettung des Jugendzentrums gehen. Ihr Vater ist nicht begeistert. Lies dir das Gespräch zunächst einmal durch. Gib dann Stück für Stück wieder, wie Becky das Gespräch am nächsten Tag ihrer Freundin erzählt.

Father: What are you going to do today?
Becky: Haven’t I told you about the protest march? They want to close down our youth club.
Father: Protest march? I don’t want you to go to a protest march when you haven’t finished your homework.
Becky: I can do it tomorrow. This march is really important for me. Tom and Chris are coming, too.
Father: Stop talking about these boys. I don’t care about them. Don’t you remember what you promised mum and me after you had shown us your school report last year?
Becky: You’re right. But I have been studying all day and I’ll do my homework tomorrow. Let me go, dad. It’s really important that a lot of people come to this protest march. Didn’t you go to the same youth club when you were young?
Father: Okay, you may go, but you have to do your homework tomorrow. When will you be back? Don’t come too late.
Becky: Thanks, dad. You’re the best. I promise I won’t be late.

Father: What are you going to do today?

Becky: Haven't I told you about the protest march? They want to close down our youth club.

Father: Protest march? I don't want you to go to a protest march when you haven't finished your homework.

Becky: I can do it tomorrow. This march is really important for me. Tom and Chris are coming, too.

Father: Stop talking about these boys. I don't care about them. Don't you remember what you promised mum and me after you had shown us your school report last year?

Becky: You're right. But I have been studying all day and I'll do my homework tomorrow. Let me go, dad. It's really important that a lot of people come to this protest march. Didn't you go to the same youth club when you were young?

Father: Okay, you may go, but you have to do your homework tomorrow. When will you be back? Don't come too late.

Becky: Thanks, dad. You're the best. I promise I won't be late.

Reading: The human right to water

A More than ten years ago, the United Nations and its organisation UNESCO reacted to growing environmental problems all over the world by adding the right to clean water to the list of human rights like freedom of speech or dignity. UNESCO played a leading role in this step. Since then, the organisation has tried to help people living in developing countries getting access to clean water which is safe for their health.

B Every person in the world has a right to clean drinking water. It should be enough water to satisfy their needs, e. g. prepare food, wash their clothes and take care of personal cleanliness. Scientists have calculated that about 50 to 100 litres of water are needed per person and day. The water should be safe to drink, which means that there mustn't be anything in it that could be dangerous for the health. The World Health Organization (WHO), another organisation of the United Nations, has developed rules and guidelines *(Richtlinien)* for countries wishing to improve their population's access to water. Another important aspect is that water should be affordable, too.

C In spite of all these targets, however, reality in developing countries often looks quite different. Some people, especially those living in the drier parts of Africa, only have access to about 10 litres of water per person and day. The main reason for that is that the water has to be carried over long distances, often more than two or three kilometres. People often have to share their drinking water with their animals or have to take it from open sources that may not be clean. As a result contagious diseases can spread very quickly. But for people living in the big cities of some developing countries the situation is hardly better: They often have to spend more money on drinking water than people living in big cities in industrialized countries.

D The proportion of the world's population living without acceptably clean drinking water is growing. This means that more and more people will have to live with less and less water. In some parts of the world water may become as valuable as gold, as it is not only used by the people themselves, but also for agriculture and in industry. This could well lead to violence or even wars for water. Some of the affected countries have already realized that the only chance they have is to work together. And even those of us living in the industrialized world should help: We should think twice before buying products whose production uses lots of water. The strawberries we buy in winter, for example, are grown in dry countries which really need the water for the population itself.

24 Lies den Text durch und ordne die Abschnitte den Überschriften zu.

_____ What is the problem?

_____ What is the situation?

_____ What might the future hold?

_____ What do the United Nations want?

25 Vervollständige die Sätze mit Informationen aus dem Text.

1. The right to clean drinking water is an important issue which has been formally accepted by ______________________________.
2. Clean drinking water is important because ______________________________ ______________________________.
3. Developing countries are supported by the WHO with ______________________________ ______________________________.
4. When people have to carry their water from sources that are kilometres away it means that ______________________________ ______________________________.
5. For people living in the big cities of developing countries the ______________________________ for water are a big problem.
6. In the future, people who don't have access to enough drinking water might ______________________________ or ______________________________.

Listening: Demonstrations 11

26 Ordne die Parolen den entsprechenden Demonstrationen zu.

1. Human rights for children! ________
2. Make society fair! ________
3. Freedom for our people! ________
4. Better jobs for mothers! ________
5. Let them learn, not work! ________
6. More money for the poor! ________
7. Put an end to child labour! ________
8. Secret police – get lost! ________
9. Equal opportunities for women! ________

Listening: New school rules 12

27 Höre dir die Unterhaltung über die Schulregeln an und trage in die Tabelle ein, welche neu und welche alt sind.

New	Old
________	________
________	________
________	________
________	________
________	________

Listening: A short history of human rights 13

28 Höre dir die Sendung an und entscheide, ob die Aussagen wahr oder falsch sind.

1. The Magna Carta is still important today.

   ☐ true ☐ false

2. Before the Magna Carta was introduced, kings had to respect the law.

   ☐ true ☐ false

3. Philosophers of the Middle Ages introduced the idea of human rights.

   ☐ true ☐ false

4. In ancient Rome, only a small part of the population was considered to have rights.

   ☐ true ☐ false

5. The colonists in America gave equal rights to Native Americans.

   ☐ true ☐ false

6. In the French Revolution, the first ever list of human rights was written down.

   ☐ true ☐ false

7. The fight for human rights turned into a tyranny in the French Revolution.

   ☐ true ☐ false

8. At the beginning of the 20th century, women campaigned for the right to work.

   ☐ true ☐ false

9. The Declaration of Human Rights was introduced by the United Nations.

   ☐ true ☐ false

Writing biographies: Georg Elser

29 Verfasse eine kurze Biografie Georg Elsers. Überlege dabei, welche der unten angegebenen Informationen du dafür verwenden kannst und welche nicht. Finde eine passende Überschrift.

Curriculum Vitae:

1903:	born in Hermaringen, Württemberg
1910–17:	school
1920s:	different jobs, travelled around
1928:	member of a Socialist party *(Partei)*
1932:	returned home, worked on parents' farm and in a factory for products needed for war
8th November 1939:	tried to kill Hitler with a bomb *(Bombe)* in Munich (not successful), arrested by police
9th April 1945:	murdered at the KZ Dachau

Interviews:

A classmate: "Georg was very clever. He was very good at making things with his hands. He was a real perfectionist and was only happy when things he had made worked as he wanted them to work. Did you know that the bomb he had built himself exploded at exactly the minute he had planned? It was real bad luck that Hitler had left the Bürgerbräukeller a few minutes earlier than expected after he had held his speech. Actually, it was strange for him to think of killing somebody as he was a very religious man. I can still remember when Georg helped to repair the tower of our church and didn't want to be paid for his work. He told the priest that he would get his payment in heaven."

A neighbour: "Oh, Georg was a very quiet and religious man. I don't think he had many close friends, but he always knew what he wanted. He often told me secretly that somebody had to stop Hitler before it was too late and he started a war. Only later did we find out that it had been Georg who had put the bomb into the Bürgerbräukeller in Munich. You can't imagine all the police and all the excitement in our small town! Georg really followed his ideas. But nobody spoke of him for years."

A fellow worker: "Georg was a really nice man although he didn't talk much. He was down to earth; a man from the village. I'm not sure if he went to church regularly but he liked nature very much and often went for long walks through the fields around our village. He was a member of a Socialist organisation, too, which was quite common for people like him who came from a working-class background. Georg tried to be fair to everybody. So the news that he had tried to kill the Führer was a strange thing for me. I still find it hard to believe that he built the bomb on his own."

Mediation: Talking about 1968

30 Vermittle in dem Gespräch zwischen deiner amerikanischen Austauschpartnerin Rachel und deinem Großvater, indem du jeweils die wichtigsten Punkte übersetzt.

Rachel: We talked about the events of the late 1960s in our history class. Our teacher told us that it was quite an exciting time all over the world. Can you tell me something about that time here in Germany?

Du: ______________________________

____

____

Großvater: Oh ja, das war eine aufregende, aber auch interessante Zeit. Ich war zwar nicht in Berlin, wo es am heißesten herging, aber auch hier bei uns war einiges los.

Du: ______________________________

____

____

Rachel: The people who protested in America protested mainly against the war in Vietnam and the segregation in the USA. But you didn't have these problems here in Germany, did you?

Du: ______________________________

____

____

Großvater: Der Vietnamkrieg spielte auch eine gewisse Rolle, aber Rassentrennung eher nicht. Bei uns ging es in erster Linie um den Generationenkonflikt. Wir wollten damals wissen, was unsere Väter in der Nazi-Zeit gemacht haben, da diese Zeit nach dem Krieg totgeschwiegen wurde.

Du: ____

____

____

Rachel: I've seen pictures of that time in Europe, with lots of people waving communist flags. How important were politics then?

Du: ____

____

____

Großvater: Die Leute, besonders die jungen Leute, waren politisch sehr interessiert und aktiv. Es wurde viel über den Sozialismus als Alternative zum bestehenden System geredet.

Du: ____

____

____

Rachel: And what effects did this all have on society in Germany?

Du: ____

____

____

Großvater: Viele der Demonstranten von damals sind dann Manager bei großen Unternehmen und Banken geworden. Trotzdem wurden Frieden und Umweltschutz wichtige Themen in der Gesellschaft.

Du: ____

____

____

Writing on an Internet forum

31 In einigen Ländern wird überlegt, das Wahlalter auf 16 Jahre herabzusetzen. Schreibe für ein internationales Onlineforum einen Beitrag mit deiner Meinung. Überlege dir dazu gut die Vor- bzw. Nachteile.

Hi guys
I live in Texas and I've grown up with guns. At the moment, we're allowed to buy a gun before we're allowed to vote. And it's the same thing with getting your driver's license. Isn't that strange? If the government says we can have guns or drive cars, it should also accept that we're responsible enough to vote.
Cowboy98, Houston, Texas

Hello everybody
I'll be 16 in a few days, but I don't think that I am prepared to vote. I mean, you need a lot of background information and although we talk a lot about such things in our social studies classes, I don't think that I have all the information I need. And there is another aspect: When I listen to my classmates, they almost sound like their parents or older brothers and sisters. They don't have an opinion of their own and are easily influenced.
Jana (15), Heidelberg, Germany

Hi there
Isn't it a fact that we have more and more old people in our society? So, who's going to represent our interests if we don't do it ourselves? They often say that young people aren't interested in politics and that we only want to have fun and go to parties. But do they care about our interests?
Jeremy (17) Leeds, UK

Talking with tolerance and respect

32 Reagiere auf folgende Situationen und zeige dabei Toleranz, Respekt oder Mut.

1. Eine blinde Frau wird am Bahnsteig angerempelt.

____

2. Ein vorbeigehender Mann beschimpft spielende Kinder.

____

3. Im Bus führt eine Frau ein lautes Gespräch am Handy.

____

4. In der Bahn hat jemand das Fenster geöffnet, obwohl es sehr kalt ist.

____

5. Im Supermarkt hat sich jemand die letzten zehn Pakete deiner Lieblingskekse genommen.

____

6. Einige Mitschüler lachen einen anderen Mitschüler aus, der eine falsche Antwort gegeben hat.

____

7. Eine Frau beschimpft eine Verkäuferin, weil sie nicht bekommt, was sie möchte.

____

Lösungen

Zoom-in

1

India	South Africa
Hindi Bollywood chicken tikka	apartheid Nelson Mandela townships
Canada	**Australia**
French-speaking population Rocky Mountains British Columbia	outback Aboriginal platypus

2

B	U	**F**	U	E	D	E	S	T	F	L
O	**Z**	**O**	**N**	**E**	**L**	**A**	**Y**	**E**	**R**	Z
G	A	**R**	**E**	**L**	**A**	**T**	**I**	**O**	**N**	**S**
V	G	**C**	**O**	**N**	**T**	**I**	**N**	**E**	**N**	**T**
E	**S**	**E**	**T**	**T**	**L**	**E**	**M**	**E**	**N**	**T**
A	I	**D**	T	G	P	A	Q	O	W	A
W	R	N	T	R	**C**	**A**	**N**	**C**	**E**	**R**

1. The **relations** between white and Aboriginal Australians have always been difficult.
2. Aboriginal families were torn apart during the **forced** and systematic relocation of indigenous people.
3. The Australian **continent** has been completely separated from the rest of the world since about 50 million years ago.
4. You can drive for hours before you reach the next **settlement**.
5. People are advised not to spend too much time in the sun. If they lie on the beach for hours, they risk getting skin **cancer**.
6. This is the result of holes in the **ozone layer**.

3 Since South Africa's **independence** in 1910 the country had been **dominated** by a white **minority**. Blacks were seen as second-class citizens in the **apartheid** system. They lived in **poverty** in **crowded** townships. However, under the **civil rights** leader Nelson Mandela black South Africans began to fight against the **racist** police state. In the free **elections** after the end of apartheid, Mandela became the first black **president**.

4
D Challenging the British
E The final step
A India as part of the British Empire
C Back home
B Gandhi develops his ideas and strategies

5 1. true; 2. false; 3. not in the text; 4. true; 5. false; 6. not in the text

6
2. Gandhi came from an **educated and rich** background.
5. Gandhi was sent to prison **several times** (so there must have been more than one judge). **All in all**, he spent eight years there.

1

Dialogue 1:

Boy: So how was your holiday in Canada?
Girl: Fantastic. We flew to Calgary. That was a good starting point. It's an amazing city, you know.
Boy: What did you do there?
Girl: Calgary has a lot of sights. We went to the top of Calgary Tower. From there you've got a unique view of the city's skyline. There are a lot of huge public squares, Olympic Plaza for example.
Boy: Weren't there Olympic Winter Games in Calgary some time ago?
Girl: Yeah, that's right. The Canada Olympic Park is not far away. We watched the National Ski Jumping competition. It was unbelievable to see the ski jumpers fly for more than 100 metres.
Boy: Did you also do any winter sports?
Girl: Of course. My parents took my brother and me to the Rocky Mountains for a week. We stayed at the Intercontinental, a very expensive hotel. We went skiing every day. That was great.

Dialogue 2:

Girl 1: Did you enjoy your trip to Canada?
Girl 2: Don't talk about it. It was terrible.
Girl 1: Really? What happened?
Girl 2: It all started with dad having trouble with his passport. It took hours before we were allowed to leave Vancouver Airport. Two days later our car was broken into. A camera was stolen. We were lucky that they didn't take mum's purse with her credit card and 300 dollars in it.
Girl 1: Oh my God.
Girl 2: That's not all. Three days before our return to Europe my brother broke his leg so he couldn't go whale watching, which is a must-do over there in Vancouver.
Girl 1: That's too bad. But did you go without him?
Girl 2: Yes, we did. It was a chance you might only get once in your life. And I really liked it. We saw some orcas. I had never before seen animals that big!
Girl 1: Bad luck for your brother.

Dialogue 3:

Boy 1: When did you come back from your holiday in Canada?
Boy 2: Oh, we arrived yesterday afternoon. I'm still pretty tired.
Boy 1: Did you like it?
Boy 2: Well … First we went to Montreal. I was surprised that most people in the street spoke French. Of course, they understood English.
Boy 1: That's funny. I didn't know that.
Boy 2: After that we drove around quite a lot. We went to the Niagara Falls on the Canadian side. We took a boat tour in the morning to see the falls from the water. That was brilliant.
Boy 1: Did you get wet?
Boy 2: Of course we did. But that was part of the fun. The rest of our holidays could have been more interesting. There were forests everywhere. You can drive for hours and see nothing but trees.
Boy 1: Did you at least stay in nice hotels?
Boy 2: No, my parents really love camping so we brought two tents in which we slept.
Boy 1: Sounds pretty boring to me. No girls except your little sister.
Boy 2: Sitting at the campfire wasn't too bad, you know. And one night there was a bear at the campsite. It was probably hungry and had smelled our meat for the barbecue. But when everyone made loud noises or shouted at it the bear ran away.

7 A: 3; B: 2; C: keiner; D: 1

8

1. Don't talk about that.	dialogue no. 2
2. Sounds pretty boring to me.	dialogue no. 3
3. Oh my God.	dialogue no. 2
4. Yeah, that's right.	dialogue no. 1
5. Bad luck.	dialogue no. 2
6. That's funny.	dialogue no. 3
7. (It) is a must-do.	dialogue no. 2
8. It was unbelievable.	dialogue no. 1

9

1. From Calgary Tower.
2. More than 100 metres.
3. The Intercontinental.
4. The girl's father.
5. A camera.
6. He broke his leg.
7. To Montreal.
8. French.
9. They made loud noises and shouted at it.

Unit 1

1

Australia as a British colony / prison	Nicknames for Australia and its people	Travelling the Great Barrier Reef
convict	Oz	natural wonder
penal colony	Aussie	sunrise tour
prisoner	down under	glass-bottom boat
criminal		World Heritage Site
judge		the world's largest coral reef system

2

1. The Great Barrier Reef **is said to be / is supposed to be** one of the best places for diving.
2. The Australian summer **is said to be / is supposed to be** very hot.
3. The relationship between Aboriginals and white Australians **is said to be / is supposed to be** difficult.
4. Sydney **is said to be / is supposed to be** very beautiful.

3

Donna could not believe what she had seen an hour ago. Her boyfriend Justin had again kissed another girl! She **was tired of** the arguments with him and **hated** the idea of meeting him in the evening. While she was thinking about the happy times with him, she **was in tears**, crying out her frustration. After half an hour her feelings turned into rage. In fact, she **was so angry** that she threw his latest present at the wall. Then the doorbell rang. Donna **was scared** that it might be Justin. She **was glad** to see that it was only the postman. When the evening came, she **felt bad**. Would she **feel confident** enough to tell Justin that it was all over? In the end she thought that she had to split up with him. After she had done it, she had mixed feelings. She **was relaxed** and happy, but she **was lonely**, too.

4 1. yummy; 2. delivered; 3. exotic; 4. barbie

5 1. aggressive; 2. racist; 3. confident; 4. ungrateful; 5. direct; 6. hypocritical; 7. shy

6

to die – death	long – length
to laugh – laughter	weak – weakness
to move – movement	silent – silence
to examine – exam(ination)	amazed – amazement

7 1. Foreshadowing; 2. Characterization; 3. Red herring; 4. Climax; 5. Point of view
Solution: When students read an English novel, they usually prefer an **adapted version**.

8
1. When Angela was young, she used to visit her granddad every day.
2. A hundred years ago most immigrants used to come from Europe.
3. I never used to like going to the theatre, but now I go once a week.
4. What did you use to do before there was the Internet?

9
1. Tracy's parents **let** her spend New Year's Eve at Bondi Beach.
2. They **made** her phone them at midnight.
3. Tracy's mum **made** her daughter call a taxi to get home safely.
4. Her little sister was disappointed because her parents **didn't let** her go.
5. Her dad **made** her stay at home because she was too young.

10
1. Blake had his party organized.
2. He had the food delivered.
3. He had the mess / the rooms cleaned.

11
1. I think I have left the door open.
2. On Saturdays dad has the car washed. / Dad has the car washed every Saturday.
3. Mum made me clean my room yesterday.
4. Leave Mark alone!
5. I (have) left my bag at school.
6. My parents didn't let me go.
7. She has her Maths homework checked / controlled by her father.
8. Let me do that!
9. The tour guide made the tourists get up early.
10. Tom had the whole story told to him.

12

1. The British, <u>whose prisons were crowded,</u> took convicts to Australia.
2. Many of those <u>who were made to do the heavy work in the new colony</u> spent the rest of their lives in Australia.
3. The first free settlers <u>who came to the penal colony</u> arrived in 1793.
4. Up to this day most Australians live at the east coast, <u>which Cook discovered first</u>.
5. Place names like Victoria or Queensland, <u>which came into use in Queen Victoria's time,</u> remind us of Australia's British past.
6. Queen Elisabeth II, <u>who is at present the British monarch</u>, is also the Queen of Australia.

13

1. Australia, **which** has the highest skin cancer rate in the world, gets very strong sunshine.
2. The huge holes in the ozone layer are a danger to people **who / that** like to spend most of their time outside.
3. The skin of people **whose** ancestors are from Europe is not adapted to the hot climate in Australia.

14

1. The immigrants **who** used to come from Europe to Australia a hundred years ago almost all come from Asia today.
2. The Aussies ______ I have met more often spend their holidays in Bali or Singapore than in Europe.
3. Their role in the Asian-Pacific world, **which** includes New Zealand and Southeast Asia, has become more important to the Australians.
4. Of course, the people ______ I talked to said that Australia's British background would never be forgotten.
5. The English language, **which** is spoken by almost all Australians, is a daily reminder of their past.
6. The sports ______ most people like are the same as in Britain: rugby and cricket are especially popular.

15

D The Aboriginal flag; B Uluru; A Rock paintings;
C Violence between whites and Aboriginals

16

1. false;	2. true;	3. false;	4. true;	5. not in the text;
6. false;	7. true;	8. true;	9. not in the text;	10. false.

17

8 White Australia apologized to the Aboriginals.
2 Aboriginals immigrated into Australia.
1 In the Dreaming the earth looked different.
4 The British discovered the Australian continent.
6 Aboriginals were taken away from their families.

3 With rock paintings Aboriginals showed their view of the world.
7 Aboriginals received the same civil rights as white Australians.
5 There were systematic killings of Aboriginals.

18 This film (2002) is based on the true story of an Aboriginal woman of the "Stolen Generations". It is set in the 1930s and begins in the small settlement of Jigalong in Western Australia. This outback town lies along the northern part of Australia's 2,000 mile-long rabbit-proof fence, which keeps wild animals off the farmland. Three part-Aboriginal children live with their family in this lonely place in the middle of nowhere. 14-year-old Molly Craig and 8-year-old Daisy Kadibil are sisters. Gracie Fields is their 10-year-old cousin.
In a dramatic scene they are taken away from their mothers and brought by force to the Moore River Settlement north of Perth, a re-education camp where they are supposed to forget their traditions and cultural identity. They have to sleep in a large room offering no privacy. They are not allowed to speak their Aboriginal language, but have to learn English so that they can work as servants to white people.
However, Molly, the strongest of the three girls, can't stand being treated like that. She loves her freedom. One day, while the other children and the white nuns are at church, Molly convinces the other two girls to run away. They want to walk back to their hometown. But not all of them are going to make it.
An Aboriginal tracker is sent after them to bring them back. Although the girls are well trained in hiding and laying false tracks, the police find out their strategy. When the girls find the rabbit-proof fence they know how to get to Jigalong. For nine weeks they walk along the fence. Strangers help them to survive by giving them food and advice.
However, when they are told that Gracie's mother is waiting for her daughter in the town of Wiluna, the girls split up. Gracie takes the way to the train station in order to go to Wiluna by train. The other two move on, but after a while they turn back to follow their cousin. They arrive at the train station only to see Gracie being caught by the police. They never see her again. Molly and Daisy continue walking along the rabbit-proof fence until they find their home. Together with their mother and grandmother they hide in the desert.

Mögliche Titel:
"(Following the) Rabbit-proof fence" (Originaltitel des Films); "Through the outback"; "Back to Jigalong"; "Away from Moore River"; "Decision at the train station"

19 Zutreffende Charaktereigenschaften sind: caring about others, self-confident, clever, brave, strong, freedom-loving.

20 Zeile 9: The family is torn apart
Zeile 16 f.: The escape
Zeile 29: Gracie is caught

21 But not all of them are going to make it. (Zeile 18 f.)

2

Shirley: Excuse me, can you help me? I am not used to all these people and this confusing traffic. Where is the Harbour Bridge?
Kyle: That's easy to find. You just go along this road until you see the Sydney Opera House and behind it there's the bridge.
Shirley: Thanks.
Kyle: Just wait a second. You said you weren't used to so many people. Where do come from?
Shirley: I live on a sheep station in the outback, about 300 miles south of Alice Springs. My dad is the boss of the station. There are about twenty people and 5,000 sheep there.
Kyle: God! That must be pretty boring.
Shirley: Oh, no! Most people say that but I love it. Everything is so quiet and peaceful out there. I couldn't live in a city like Sydney where there's so much noise the whole day.
Kyle: I guess you get used to it. I have been living in the city for almost all my life. In fact, I live in a small apartment right around the corner together with my parents and my little sister Sue. It's in the skyscraper you can see over there.
Shirley: I couldn't live like that. It looks so narrow and crowded. We've got so much space on our farm. My own room is very big.
Kyle: Have you got any brothers and sisters?
Shirley: No, that's a pity. But I know everyone out there very well – I mean the workers and their wives – and we are almost like a big family.
Kyle: I'd feel very lonely. But I guess you've got some friends from school that you meet every day?
Shirley: No, there's no school anywhere near the sheep station. My school is the School of the Air. My teacher is in Alice Springs and my classmates are some hundred miles away, too. With my laptop I can chat with them. All of them have webcams so we see each other, too. I don't have to sit in a classroom all day. Sometimes I take the computer outside and sit somewhere under a tree while I'm doing my work.
Kyle: That means that you can't meet your friends every day?

Shirley: No, that's impossible. We meet about three or four times a year.
Kyle: But what do you do after school, after you've done your homework? Don't you miss spending your time with hobbies like sports? For example, I play the guitar and I've got lessons every Tuesday. And what about Friday nights? I love going to the disco!
Shirley: Of course I've got hobbies! I love riding. Dad bought me my own horse and I'm free to ride anywhere I like. And what's best of all: I am allowed to ride his motorbike, which is great fun.
Kyle: Maybe it's not too bad living in the outback after all. What's your name?
Shirley: Shirley.
Kyle: I'm Kyle. Are you on Facebook?

22

Pro	Con
It is quiet and peaceful.	It is boring.
There is a lot of space. Shirley has got a big room.	It is lonely. There are no friends to meet.
Shirley doesn't have to sit in a classroom all day. She can do her work outside with her laptop.	It is difficult to spend time with hobbies like sports or music lessons.
Shirley has the freedom to ride where she likes. She is allowed to use her dad's motorbike.	There is no opportunity to go to a disco.

23 **Shirley**: Her father is the boss of a sheep station about 300 miles south of Alice Springs in the outback. There are twenty people working for him who she regards as her family. She has no brothers and sisters.
Kyle: He lives in a small flat in a skyscraper in Sydney where he has lived for almost all his life. He's got a little sister named Sue.

3

Tracy: Hi, I'm Tracy Jones. Would you have some time to answer a few questions? I really want to find out more about the Royal Flying Doctor Service. I'd like to write an article about it for our school magazine.
Doctor: Yeah, come in.
Tracy: Well, I wonder how it all began. Can you tell me something about the beginnings of the service?

Doctor: Of course. It all started in 1928 with a single base in Queensland. But in the 1930s and 40s more and more bases were founded so that the Flying Doctors could offer their service in the whole of the outback. Today we've got 61 planes on 21 starting and landing bases throughout the country.
Tracy: How many people depend on your service?
Doctor: Well, about 270,000 people have no doctor to go to so they call us. We provide medical care for an area of almost 7 million square kilometres. That's nearly the size of the USA.
Tracy: That's amazing. How many people call you every day?
Doctor: In 2012 we had 750 phone calls daily on average. However, we did not fly to all of them.
Tracy: What kind of help did you give them?
Doctor: It's mostly about calming people down. Often someone has been hurt and people are afraid that it might get serious. So we ask them a lot of questions trying to find out whether they could care for the patients themselves. Very often they simply need someone who tells them what to do.
Tracy: But how do they get the necessary medicine?
Doctor: On isolated farms the Flying Doctors have put up boxes with medicines. Over the phone we can tell people what to take.
Tracy: And how often do you actually fly out into the middle of nowhere?
Doctor: Last year we had 112 flights every day, adding up to more than 40,000 flights a year. We start our planes when we actually need to bring people from the outback to a hospital.
Tracy: If there is an emergency, how long does it take the Flying Doctors to get there?
Doctor: It usually doesn't take more than two hours. In most cases we are there within an hour.
Tracy: For how long have you been working for the Flying Doctors?
Doctor: I have been working here for about nine years now. It is quite interesting. Every day is different. You don't know what's going to come up next.
Tracy: Thank you for your time.
Doctor: No problem.

24
1. Queensland
2. 270,000 people
3. tell people how to help themselves.
4. 112 people
5. 120 minutes
6. It is different every day.

4

Travel agent:	What can I do for you?
Man:	Well, we arrived in Sydney two days ago. Now we would like to plan our next four weeks in Australia in more detail.
Woman:	We've got some ideas but maybe you can help us to sort things out.
Travel agent:	Sure. What are you interested in?
Man:	Natural sights …
Woman:	… and animals. Some cultural highlights and …
Man:	We also want to spend some time on the beach …
Travel agent:	Okay. Okay. If I were you, I would fly from Sydney to Alice Springs. There you could do a three-day tour through the Red Centre of Australia, that's Uluru, which is known as Ayers Rock, the Olgas and King's Canyon: amazing red rocks which are most impressive at sunset. Quite an adventure in the outback, but perfectly organized.
Man:	Yeah, that sounds great.
Travel agent:	From Alice Springs I would take a camper and travel north. There are some campsites on your way, but you mustn't forget to take enough water and food with you at all times.
Woman:	Are there no shops?
Travel agent:	Well, you might have to drive for about 150 kilometres until you reach the next shop. Altogether it's 1,483 kilometres on the Stuart Highway before you reach Darwin.
Woman:	Are there any interesting sights on the way?
Travel agent:	You should stop at Katherine Gorge where you can do a canoe tour. Then you definitely shouldn't miss Kakadu National Park with its famous wildlife. The park offers boat tours on which you can see crocodiles and other Australian animals. You can also take trips to the most famous Aboriginal rock paintings where you can learn a lot about the culture of the indigenous people.
Man:	Really? How interesting. And once we are in Darwin, what can we do there?
Travel agent:	If I were you, I would fly to Cairns in Queensland. That's the ideal place to spend some days on the beach. Maybe you would like to go diving on the Great Barrier Reef?
Woman:	Definitely. That's a must. Is there a place where we can learn to dive?
Travel agent:	Oh, not only one. There are lots of diving schools along the coast. You should allow at least four days for the lessons and three days for the trip to the Great Barrier Reef. The reef is 2,600 kilometres long and is home to 1,500 species of fish. So there's plenty to see.

Man:	Is it warm enough at this time of the year?
Travel agent:	It's quite cold here in Sydney right now because it is winter, but in Queensland it is hot. In the north temperatures usually stay above 30° C. If you've got even more time, you could explore the Cape York Peninsula, which is the most northern part of Queensland. There you could visit Cooktown where James Cook landed when he discovered Australia. Or you could drive south along the coast back to Sydney. But that would take you about two days. So perhaps you would prefer to take the plane back.
Woman:	Yeah, I think we are going to do that. Thank you very much!

25

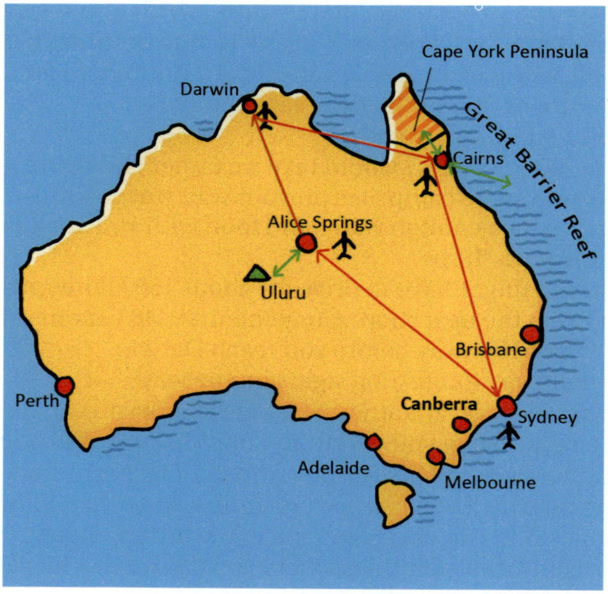

26

1. King's Canyon is in the **Red Centre** of Australia.
2. **The Stuart Highway** connects Alice Springs and Darwin.
3. Kakadu National Park is famous for **its Aboriginal rock paintings**.
4. The Great Barrier Reef is **2,600** kilometres long.
5. In the Australian winter it is **hot** in Queensland.
6. Cooktown is **north** of Cairns.

5

Police Officer: Can I help you?
Man: Yeah, someone has stolen my rucksack with my credit card and my mobile phone.
Police Officer: Well, we should fill in one of these forms. What's your name?
Man: Harald Steinmeyer.
Police Officer: Could you please spell your last name? What was that again?
Man: Steinmeyer. S – T – E – I – N – M – E – Y – E – R.
Police Officer: You are a tourist, aren't you? Where do you live?
Man: Do you mean my home address?
Police Officer: Yes.
Man: It's Hermannstraße number 13 in 70178 Stuttgart. That's in Germany.
Police Officer: Is that the town where the Porsche cars come from?
Man: Yeah, that's it.
Police Officer: Okay. When and where was your rucksack stolen?
Man: It happened this afternoon at about 2 o'clock.
Police Officer: Right. It's Tuesday, the 20th of August 2012.
Man: My wife and I had lunch in one of the restaurants at the top of Sydney Tower. I went to the toilet for a minute and when I came back, the rucksack was gone. My wife hadn't seen anything.
Police Officer: What did the backpack look like? And what was in it? I have to put that down as well.
Man: It was a black backpack, standard size, with a little tag from the local football club VfB Stuttgart. It's red and white. There was a grey pullover in it, my credit card and about 100 Australian dollars. Last but not least my mobile phone.
Police Officer: Well, we'll do our best to find the thief, of course. But usually chances are not really good to get the stolen money back. Please call us in five days. Then we can tell you more. Here's our phone number.

27

Sydney Police Department

Last name: Steinmeyer First name: Harald
Street: Hermannstr. 13 City: Stuttgart /Germany Postcode: 70178

Date / Time of the crime: Tuesday, 20 August 2012, 2 pm

Location of the crime: Restaurant at the top of Sydney Tower

Description: A black backpack with a red and white tag (from the local football club VfB Stuttgart) was stolen. There were a credit card, 100 Australian dollars in cash, a mobile phone and a grey pullover in it.

28 *Musterlösung*

Dear Mum,
it's our third week in Australia. Times passes by very quickly as there is so much to see. After a road trip from Alice Springs to Darwin we flew to Cairns. We took some diving lessons before we went to the Great Barrier Reef for three days. The underwater world is fantastic. We even saw reef sharks. I was a little scared although they are not dangerous. The Aussies we met are very nice. Especially the people on the boat were pretty cool.
See you soon

Das sollte in deiner Lösung enthalten sein:

- ☐ Anrede und Grußformel
- ☐ alle Elemente aus den Reisenotizen
- ☐ ein paar subjektive Eindrücke

29 *Musterlösung*

Ladies and Gentlemen, black and white fellow citizens,
today is the day of truth. Today is the day on which we accept our mistakes. Today is the day on which we say sorry to the Aboriginal people. We have to apologize for showing no respect towards their unique culture. We have to apologize for trying to destroy them. And we have to apologize for taking children of mixed race away from their mothers and fathers, from their homes and their families.
40 years ago this was stopped, but it has not been forgotten by the Stolen Generations. For 40 years white Australia just looked away and said nothing. It was not easy to face the fact that our actions were racist. We had no right to do as we did.

But here I stand as Prime Minister and as a white Australian to admit that we have been wrong and to officially apologize to the Aborigines.
It will take time, maybe another generation, to heal the wounds. But we should start tomorrow or even today to shake hands. It is our duty to create a united Australia, in which every group is welcome. Be part of our common future.

Das sollte in deiner Lösung enthalten sein:

- ☐ Anrede an alle Australier, insbesondere aber an die Aborigines
- ☐ Eingeständnis, dass Fehler gemacht wurden
- ☐ Rückblick: Bezug auf Diskriminierung und die Stolen Generations
- ☐ Entschuldigung mit Begriffen wie „apologize“, „sorry“
- ☐ positiver Blick in die Zukunft: Versöhnung der ethnischen Gruppen

30 *Musterlösung*

Helpers in the middle of nowhere: A portrait of the Royal Flying Doctor Service
Since 1928 the Royal Flying Doctor Service, usually called the Flying Doctors, has been giving medical care to people in the Australian outback. With their 61 planes, the Flying Doctors care for more than 270,000 people on isolated farms, in the desert and the rainforests. Most of the time they tell people on the phone how they can help themselves. Medicine can be taken from boxes put up by the Flying Doctors. In an emergency it takes the Flying Doctors less than two hours to get there and transport the patients to a hospital somewhere in Australia.

Das sollte in deiner Lösung enthalten sein:

- ☐ Überschrift, die klar sagt, worum es geht, aber auch Interesse weckt
- ☐ Antwort auf die Frage: Wer sind die Flying Doctors? (gleich zu Beginn)
- ☐ Interessante Fakten zur Geschichte und / oder Arbeitsweise des Service

Unit 2

1 1. meteorologist; 2. nurse; 3. (fashion) model; 4. firefighter; 5. hairdresser; 6. gardener; 7. architect; 8. musician

2 1. money: banker; 2. education: teacher; 3. law: lawyer / judge; 4. magazines: editor / journalist; 5. politics: politician / journalist; 6. cakes: baker; 7. food: cook / baker / waiter / waitress; 8. medicine: doctor / nurse

3

S						G			
T	R	A	I	N		C			
U	N	I	V	E	R	S	I	T	Y
D		A	L	E	V	E	L	S	
Y		E	X	A	M	S			

Lösungswort: **Cambridge**

4 If you want to apply for a **placement**, a **part-time** or a full-time job, your letter of application should have no spelling mistakes. As there is a lot of **competition**, a letter with spelling mistakes will be thrown away at once. Sometimes there is a **deadline** so don't be late with your application. If you are lucky, you will get an **invitation** for an **interview**. The **personnel manager** will ask you about your qualifications and whether you have got any **work experience**. You should also ask questions about the company. To prepare for the interview, you should check **the company's website**. The interview is very important, so you should try to **make a good impression** on the interviewer. He will not only listen to what you're saying but will notice your **body language**, too. So look confident and smile. The interviewer will not tell you right away whether you have got the job. But perhaps the **employer** will phone you a couple of days later.

5

1. Only students **having** top marks in their A-levels can go to Oxford or Cambridge University.
2. Sam took the training course in computer programming **expected** from future IT students.
3. Parents **worried** about their children's future should talk with them about the pros and cons of their chosen careers.
4. Students **interested** in studying in the USA should look at the universities' websites.

6

1. Schüler, die sich über verschiedene Karrieremöglichkeiten informieren möchten, sollten das Connexions Centre aufsuchen.
2. Schüler, die zu einem Vorstellungsgespräch eingeladen sind, sollten einige Fragen vorbereiten.
3. Menschen, die schon lange arbeitslos sind, haben oft Schwierigkeiten, einen neuen Job zu finden.
4. Der Personalchef schaute sich den Lebenslauf an, der dem Bewerbungsschreiben beigefügt war.

7

1. **Coming** into the waiting room, Michael was surprised to see his old girlfriend as a nurse.
2. **Studying** at York University, he hadn't seen her for a few years.
3. **Looking at her**, he didn't know what to say.
4. **Standing** there, he felt bad.

8

Leaving school after my GCSEs, I had no idea which career to choose. **Having to do something**, I did a training course in business. I didn't finish it but it took some time before I found out what I really wanted. (**While**) **working as a waitress**, I realized that dealing with people wasn't really my thing. So instead, **having always felt happy outdoors**, I tried a placement with a gardening company. Now I can enjoy the beauty of nature **while working as a gardener**.

9

1. **Having sounded** very interesting in the advert, the training course turned out to be disappointing.
2. **Having known** what I wanted to do since my 15th birthday, I am going to apply for a job as a meteorologist tomorrow.
3. **Having been trained** as a waiter, I now want to open a café.

10

1. We stopped for a minute and listened to a musician **performing** his song.
2. Marco saw Peter **working** in the fish and chips shop when he went by.
3. Blake looked up and suddenly noticed his classmate **copying** his homework.
4. I watched my little sister **drop** her bowl of cornflakes on the floor.

5. He didn't hear the young man **say** goodbye because he quickly shut the door.
6. When Sue came home she saw her dad **sitting** in his chair and **reading** the newspaper.
7. Alena watched the thief **run** away until he disappeared around the corner.

11 *Du*: Yeah, that's right. There was a huge crowd. She was watching people **come** and **go**.
Du: She noticed the young man **watching** the Asian tourist. He sat / was sitting there without looking at anything else.
Du: She didn't see him **take** the camera because she was looking somewhere else at that exact moment. But she saw him **running** away quickly and heard the Asian woman **shouting** for help.

12
1. I'**m going to** spend my summer holidays in Italy.
2. Next Saturday I **will be** 16.
3. Look at the dark clouds. It's going to rain soon.
4. Derrick **will probably get** a place at Christ Church College.
5. If I get an A in Maths, Barclay's Bank **will offer** me a job.

13
1. Are you coming with us tonight? – No, I **am watching** the football game on TV at 8.45 pm.
2. The concert **begins** at 7.30 pm.
3. Would you believe it! Mark **is taking** Sue out for dinner tomorrow night.
4. The plane **lands** in Frankfurt at 9.15 am.
5. The train **leaves** Waterloo Station at midnight.
6. Next Sunday Donna **is helping** her mum prepare the birthday party.
7. Hurry up! The English lesson **starts** at 10.30.
8. I **am going** to Paris next weekend.

14 On Monday he is presenting his History project. At 2 pm on Tuesday he is having his bike repaired at Mario's bike shop. At 4 pm on Wednesday he is watching his mum on TV. At 11.30 am on Thursday he is having an interview at The Sports Shop. On Friday he is going on a date with Caitlin at 7.30 pm.

15
Mya: I really don't know what to do after leaving school. But I'**m meeting** my personal adviser at the Connexions centre tomorrow.
Megan: I'**m going to study** at university. I **won't make** it into Oxford or Cambridge, but perhaps I'**ll get** a place at York or Leicester. And then **I'm going to be** a lawyer one day. But anyway, about tonight: What **are you going to wear**?
Mya: I thought of my new pink T-shirt.

Megan: Oh, look, I'**ll give** you my new ring to wear with it. When shall we meet?
Mya: The train **leaves** at 7.05 pm. Let's meet at ten to seven.
Megan: You're always late. Tonight probably **won't be** any different! **Will** you please **call** me if you aren't on time?

16 A Three schools or one for all; D Languages; E University and career; C Repeating a year; B Students' social backgrounds

17 1. true; 2. not in the text; 3. true; 4. not in the text; 5. not in the text; 6. false; 7. not in the text; 8. true; 9. true

18
5 Steve lost his job at Apple.
3 He went to India.
10 He quit his job with Apple.
1 Steve went to Reed College.
7 Apple had lost almost all its money.
4 Steve worked for Atari.
6 He bought Pixar.
8 The iPod was invented.
2 Steve had to sleep on the floor because he had no money.
9 Apple revolutionized the mobile phone.

19
1. The person who introduced Steve to the world of electronics was **his father**.
2. Atari is famous for **computer games**.
3. Steve founded Apple **in his parents' garage**.
4. The first Macintosh computer already had a mouse.
5. Steve and Pixar won Oscars for **Best Animated Feature**.
6. The invention of the iPod went along with **the introduction of iTunes**.
7. Steve Jobs died at the age of **56**.
8. As CEO of Apple Steve earned **only $ 1 a year**.

20 D Founding the Missionaries of Charity; A The call of God; C Teaching in a convent school in Calcutta; B Learning English; E The Nobel Peace Prize

21 1. false; 2. true; 3. false; 4. not in the text; 5. false; 6. true; 7. true; 8. true; 9. not in the text; 10. false; 11. true. 12. not in the text

22

1. Mother Teresa was born **in Skopje**.
3. She joined the Sisters of **Loreto**.
5. She first taught in a school in **Darjeeling**.
10. She won the Nobel Peace Prize **for her life-long fight against poverty**.

23

Zeilen 3–5:	Agnes' mother told her religious stories.
Zeile 13 f.:	Agnes started calling herself Teresa.
Zeile 20 f.:	She was not sure whether she had chosen the right way.
Zeile 21 f.:	For whom do the Missionaries of Charity care?
Zeilen 26–28:	Mother Teresa thought that education for the poor was very important.

6

Sylvia: Hi, Donovan.
Donovan: Hi, Sylvia. How are you?
Sylvia: Fine. What about you?
Donovan: I'm okay. Well, to tell you the truth, I keep worrying about what to do after my GCSEs. I just don't know whether I should stay at school for my A-levels.
Sylvia: Have you got any idea what kind of job you'd like to have?
Donovan: I did two weeks of work experience at our local bakery but I hated it from the beginning. I had to get up at 4 o'clock in the morning. But I still want to do something practical. So I thought – maybe – I'd like to become a hairdresser.
Sylvia: I couldn't do that but it suits you.
Donovan: I know it's not the best-paid job but you're in contact with people and you have to be creative.
Sylvia: I don't want to put you off, but have you thought of a hairdresser's image in society?
Donovan: No. I know that people often believe that male hairdressers are homosexual but I think image is not important. You have to be happy in what you do. One of the good things in that business is that you can open your own hairdresser's shop after a few years.
Sylvia: You've got your head in the clouds! It takes at least 15 years to work your way up to earn enough money to do that.
Donovan: Never mind. It is still possible.
Sylvia: Okay, okay.
Donovan: Have you already decided what you are going to do?
Sylvia: Oh yeah. I have always wanted to become an architect – like my dad. He organised this year's work experience on a construction site for me. I really liked it. Talking to the builder and the architect I was able to get a good idea of what it's like. It really makes you happy if a house that you designed gets built.

Donovan: That's a good job. However, it takes many years before you earn your own money.
Sylvia: Yeah, I know. My parents will have to support me through school and university for the next six or seven years. But once I start working I'll earn quite a lot.
Donovan: That's true. What I wouldn't like about the job as an architect is that you always have to meet deadlines.
Sylvia: Oh yeah, that's quite annoying. You've got no fixed working hours. When you have to finish a project, you might have to work through the night to get it done.

24

	Sylvia	Donovan
Work experience (plus comment)	– on a construction site – helpful to get a better idea of the job	– in a bakery – bad job because you have to get up early
Career as	architect	hairdresser
Pros	– it makes you happy to see a house built that you designed – well-paid job	– in contact with people – creative – you can open your own hairdresser's shop
Cons	– it takes a long time before you become independent / earn your own money – no fixed working hours because you often have to meet deadlines	– not the best-paid job – negative image

25 Sylvia: 2; 3; 5; 7.
Donovan: 1; 4; 6.

7

Interview 1
Interviewer: Hello, Mr Warner.
Ryan: Nice to meet you.
Interviewer: Take a seat.
Ryan: Thank you.
Interviewer: Did you come all the way down from York today?
Ryan: Yeah. It's just a two-hour journey by train. It wasn't too bad.

Interviewer:	My wife used to live in York before we moved to London. She lived very close to the Cathedral in King's Road.
Ryan:	Well, that's just around the corner from where I live. Oxford St., number 10.
Interviewer:	Let's go through your CV again. Ryan Warner, born in Scarborough. You're in your final year at York University where you're doing History. I see that you've done two placements. Both of them were with "The Sun". You know that "The Sun" is quite a different newspaper compared to "The Times".
Ryan:	Yeah, that's true. I knew that you were going to ask me that question. The thing is that my uncle knew someone there. That's the reason why I got these placements.
Interviewer:	How would you characterize the difference between "The Sun" and "The Times"?
Ryan:	"The Sun" always looks for sensations and tragedies. And their style of writing is very different to "The Times" as well: always big headlines and short texts. "The Times" is a serious newspaper, critical but not in favour of a special political party. That's why I am here.
Interviewer:	I see that your English mark at school wasn't really brilliant.
Ryan:	Yeah, you're right. I just wasn't good at analysing Shakespeare in class tests and so I got only a B. But I think writing for a newspaper is different. It's another type of text. You have to be exact. You only have a number of lines to express what you want to say.
Interviewer:	That's definitely true. Do you read a lot, I mean, just for fun?
Ryan:	Oh yeah. I prefer non-fiction books, for example on politics, to novels. I think you can only be a good writer if you read a lot.
Interviewer:	I agree with that. Well, have you got any questions?
Ryan:	I understood from the advertisement that you're looking for a journalist for the northern part of the UK. Which area would I have to write about?
Interviewer:	That would include Yorkshire, Scotland, even Northern Ireland.
Ryan:	Mmh … To tell you the truth, I don't really like being away over night but I think that could be arranged.
Interviewer:	Well, you're just 21. That shouldn't be a problem.
Ryan:	Well, of course not. But my mother is handicapped and often needs help.
Interviewer:	Oh, I see.
Ryan:	There's another question I'd like to ask: Is there a possibility of working down here in London in some years' time?

Interviewer: Of course there is. I can't promise you anything but if you do a good job, you might end up being the editor. – I think we can stop here. You'll hear from me before the end of the month. Thanks for coming.

Ryan: Thank you for inviting me to this interview.

Interview 2

Interviewer: Hello, Ms Stirling.

Megan: Hello.

Interviewer: Take a seat.

Megan: *(sits down without saying thank you).*

Interviewer: So you're from Cornwall.

Megan: Yeah.

Interviewer: We spent our summer holidays there two years ago. We really loved it.

Megan: It's nice.

Interviewer: Well, let's go through your CV. Megan Stirling, 15, Harbour Road, Bristol, aged 23. After your A-levels you started a course in law but you didn't finish that.

Megan: Yeah, that's true. It was a mistake to begin that. My parents wanted me to do it but after a year I began to realize that I wanted to do something different.

Interviewer: Then you did a training course to become a nurse. Do you have any writing experience?

Megan: At school I was one of the best in my class in English. You can see that from my school report.

Interviewer: Yeah, you had an A. But I mean, did you do any placements with a newspaper?

Megan: No, but I worked for the school magazine for some years.

Interviewer: Why do you want to work for "The Times"?

Megan: Ehm. – Well, I saw the advert …

Interviewer: Have you got any questions you'd like to ask?

Megan: Not really. – Or maybe: how much money would I earn at the beginning?

Interviewer: It depends on you. The more you write for us, the more you get.

Megan: I see.

Inteviewer: I think we can stop here. You'll hear from me by the end of the month. Thanks for coming.

Megan: Okay.

26 **Interview 1:**
positive: The applicant has done two placements. In the interview he was well prepared, informed about the difference between "The Sun" and "The Times". He asked good questions about the job. He was also very friendly. He reads a lot.
negative: His English mark was not brilliant. His mobility is limited.

Interview 2:
positive: The applicant worked for the school magazine for some years. At school she was one of the best in English.
negative: She had no work experience in paid journalism (for example placements). It seemed as if she hadn't thought about why she wanted to apply for the job with "The Times". Her only question was about money. She was impolite. She didn't seem to know what she wanted (various courses).

27

	Applicant 1	Applicant 2
Name	Ryan Warner	Megan Stirling
Address	10, Oxford St. York	15, Harbour Rd. Bristol
Age	21	23

28 *Musterlösung*

1. Be polite. Say thank you when you are offered a seat und thank the interviewer when you leave.
2. Answer questions with more than yes or no.
3. Be well-informed about the job. Check the company's website. Explain why you applied for that job and why you are the right person for it.
4. Ask questions about training, career etc. You may ask about money, but don't start with that!
5. Don't speak too casually.

Das sollte in deiner Lösung enthalten sein:

- ☐ Du nimmst Bezug auf einige der Negativpunkte, die du in Übung 27 herausgearbeitet hast, und machst Verbesserungsvorschläge.
- ☐ Die Themen Höflichkeit und Informiertheit sollten vorkommen.

29 *Musterlösung*

Mr Ryan Warner
10 Oxford St.
York

Personnel Manager
"The Times"
London

15 August 2013

Your application

Dear Mr Warner

Having made a very good impression in the interview, you will be pleased to hear that we would like to offer you the job as a journalist for the northern UK.

If you would like to accept our offer, please sign the contract and send it back to us. We look forward to your reply.

Yours sincerely

Walter Riverdale
Walter Riverdale

Encl. Contract

Das sollte in deiner Lösung enthalten sein:

- ☐ Adressen, Datum
- ☐ Anrede und Abschiedsformel
- ☐ Höfliche Wendungen wie „look forward to", „would like to"
- ☐ Die Betreffzeile zeigt auf den ersten Blick, worum es geht.
- ☐ Das Schreiben nimmt Bezug auf das Vorstellungsgespräch.
- ☐ Keine Umgangssprache, keine Kurzformen

30 *Musterlösung*

Bournemouth Tourist
Information Centre
Westover Rd., Bournemouth
Dorset BH1 2BU
United Kingdom

Im Kirchacker 13
79115 Freiburg/Breisgau
Germany

12 February 2013

Application: German-speaking assistant for the summer holidays

Dear Sir or Madam

I am writing to apply for the summer job at the Bournemouth Tourist Information Centre advertised in the *Allgemeines Abendblatt.*

I am 16 years old and attending grade 10 of Ludwig-Uhland-Gymnasium in Freiburg. I really enjoy working with people and would very much like to give tourists assistance and information so that they will remember their wonderful holiday in Bournemouth. My father has a little travel agency where I sometimes help out. So I know how to deal with customers looking for a hotel, for example. My English is quite good (B+) as you can see from my last school report. This means that I could be of help to English-speaking tourists.

I visited the United Kingdom two years ago when my parents took me to London. After that we spent two weeks in Cornwall. As I have always loved the English language and culture, I would like to get to know the people and the country better. A summer job at the Tourist Information Centre would be an ideal opportunity for that.

I hope very much that you are able to offer me this work experience during the summer holidays. I look forward to hearing from you.

Yours sincerely

Michael König
Michael König

Encl. CV, school reports

Das sollte in deiner Lösung enthalten sein:

- ☐ Adressen, Datum
- ☐ Anrede und Abschiedsformel
- ☐ Das Wort „application“ sollte in der Betreffzeile auftauchen.
- ☐ Du nimmst Bezug auf die Anzeige.
- ☐ Du schreibst etwas darüber, warum du dich für diese Stelle interessierst und besonders dafür geeignet bist (z. B. Qualifikation, Fähigkeiten, Erfahrungen).
- ☐ Du erwähnst Anhänge wie Lebenslauf oder Zeugnisse.
- ☐ Keine Umgangssprache, keine Kurzformen

Revision A

1 Film review.

2

Title:	Australia		
Category:	Historical romance		
Running time:	165 min	Year:	2008
Director:	Baz Luhrmann		
Cast: (actors / role)	Nicole Kidman (Lady Sarah Ashley) Hugh Jackman (Drover) Brandon Walters (Nullah)		
Awards: (nominations and wins)	Academy Award (Oscar) for Costume Design (nominated) Australian Critics Award: Best Supporting Actor (won)		
Rating in the review:	4 (out of 5) stars		

3 Facts: 1; 2; 3; 6; 9.
Opinion: 4; 5; 7; 8.

4
1. The film was produced in the **USA and Australia**.
2. Lady Ashley's farm is called **Faraway Downs**.
3. King Carney is **unfair** to Lady Ashley.
4. The plot ends in the year **1942**.
5. The story is **romantic**.

5 *Musterlösung*

Hi Todd
IT Solutions is a company which does business all over the world. They provide all leading car manufacturers with electronics.
The company is looking for a male or female project manager to develop a computer-based warning system for cars in dangerous traffic situations.
The project manager will lead an international team of 25 engineers and IT specialists.
The applicant should have studied IT and should have some work experience. He / she should be used to develop his / her own ideas.
He / she should speak fluent English in order to communicate within the company and with its world-wide partners. He / she should have no problems with working in other countries for several months each year.
Apply to Herr Müller (see address) before the deadline (May 22) !
Take care
Lisa

Unit 3

1 Surprisingly, teenagers today don't spend as much time as their parents in front of the **television**. Instead, most teenagers prefer surfing the **Internet**. They use it as a **source** of information and entertainment. But **social networking sites** have the greatest **influence** on teenagers' lives these days. The **advertising** industry has reacted to the time spent online and has created Internet **commercials** especially for teenagers. Today, people have access to a lot of media using their **mobile phones**: they can **download** music, exchange photos or videos and send **text messages** to their friends all at the same time. However, even in this **digital** world there are still lots of people who read **printed** media like magazines or newspapers.

2 Anweisung: direction; Dämmerlicht: soft lighting; Totale: wide shot; heranfahren / heranzoomen: zoom in; Nahaufnahme: close-up; Halbnahe: medium shot; Hintergrundkommentar: voice-over; Regisseur: director; Drehbuch: film script; schneiden: cut; Einstellung / Ansicht: view

M	**F**	O	R	M	**V**	A	A	D	D	E	R	T	U	V
O	**I**	V	O	N	**I**	U	M	**Z**	M	I	M	I	P	O
T	**L**	**W**	**I**	**D**	**E**	**S**	**H**	**O**	**T**	Z	U	I	O	U
H	**M**	E	T	H	**W**	B	M	**O**	S	D	F	R	E	A
V	**S**	A	P	P	E	L	R	**M**	E	R	N	L	R	T
O	**C**	H	**S**	**O**	**F**	**T**	**L**	**I**	**G**	**H**	**T**	**I**	**N**	**G**
I	**R**	E	R	H	J	L	B	**N**	N	F	E	G	A	I
C	**I**	M	A	U	S	**D**	G	J	K	M	F	H	E	R
E	**P**	T	**M**	**E**	**D**	**I**	**U**	**M**	**S**	**H**	**O**	**T**	O	M
O	**T**	E	W	A	S	**R**	R	T	R	Z	U	I	O	P
V	R	**C**	**L**	**O**	**S**	**E**	**U**	**P**	P	E	N	N	I	N
E	T	O	P	F	D	**C**	E	C	K	E	L	G	U	M
R	**D**	**I**	**R**	**E**	**C**	**T**	**I**	**O**	**N**	A	U	T	O	O
I	Z	R	E	N	B	**O**	R	T	U	N	H	D	F	R
C	**U**	**T**	R	U	N	**R**	T	Z	I	P	P	O	R	E

3

1. The show was so **exciting** that I forgot the time. You could feel the **excitement** of the audience. Everybody was very **excited**.
2. I found the **summarized** plot of the book on the Internet. I can't **summarize** texts very well. I always get bad marks for my **summaries**.
3. They **surprised** us with their visit last week. The **surprised** children stood there with their mouths open. This was a real **surprise**.
4. **Write** more clearly, please. You risk bad marks in your **written** tests if the teacher can't read your hand**writing**.
5. The **speaker** was brilliant. He **spoke** without any accent. His **speech** was very interesting.

4

I like the Internet **because** I love chatting with my friends on social networking sites. Some time ago my grandma also wanted to go online **so that** she could keep in touch with the world. **As a result** my grandma spends more and more time in front of the computer, even more than I do. **Because of that** my grandpa started to write to her on Facebook when he wanted to tell her something. **Since** she agrees that this is a stupid situation, they have decided to use the Internet less often.

5

1. The fridge is **almost** empty.
2. Paul ran / was running as **fast** as he could.
3. In my **opinion** you are right.
4. What is the **meaning** of this word? / What does this word **mean**?
5. When do I **get** my money back?
6. The lack of women is **becoming** a problem in China.

6

Eigene Meinung	Widerspruch
I'm sure	you can't say that
I believe	I see that differently
in my opinion	I disagree
it seems to me	that's not true
	I think you're wrong

7

Sally: I **like** rap. The lyrics **are** very important for me.
Carol: Oh no, I **think** rap music is too aggressive. I sometimes even **feel** frightened. I've just seen a hip-hop dance group on TV, and now **I'm planning** to join one. I really **love** hip-hop and I **wish** I could dance like the stars in the music videos.

Jo: We **are doing** a school project on Mozart at the moment. I **know** it **sounds** boring, but now I **want** to go to the opera.
Frank: I **prefer** rock music to any other kind of music. My dad **plays** in a 1980s-style band. Look, I **am wearing** their band T-shirt.

8
1.The tourists **are** in the coach.
2. Stop it! You **are being** silly.
3. Charles **has** got a new mobile.
4. We **are having** breakfast.
5. She **is feeling** her way to the door.
6. I **don't feel** well today.

9
Hi Steve
I'**ve been seeing** Leonie for three months now. I **think** she is my great love. We do a lot of things together. We **went** to a concert last Friday and we enjoyed it very much. I brought her home after that. We were standing in front of her house and I **was holding** her close as it **was** cold. Suddenly she gave me a kiss.
We're loving every minute of being together and when we **aren't** together, we **text** each other all the time. Some of my friends **believe** that I'm being silly, but they don't understand. I **feel** happy when we're together. On the other hand I don't mean to ignore them totally. I **love** everything about Leonie. Her hair smells wonderful, she **wears** nice jeans and she looks just beautiful. I'**m thinking** of asking her to go to the cinema next Saturday. There's a film we **haven't seen** yet. I hope she **has** time because she's doing an important project at school at the moment. Oh, my mobile'**s ringing**. Maybe it's Leonie.
See you, Max

10
One night my phone rang. **Not for a moment did I think** that this phone call would change my life forever. When I answered the phone a voice said, "It's Bill Gates speaking." **Never / Not in my wildest dreams would I have believed** this, so I simply said, "Stop joking."
But the man went on to tell me he had heard of my work as a computer engineer and wanted to offer me a job.
I was having breakfast the next morning when I got an e-mail. **Not for one moment did I think** that this mail might have something to do with the phone call the night before. But Bill Gates made me the same offer again. **Not only was I surprised**, but also very excited. **Never would I have thought** that such a dream could come true.
So I arranged a meeting at his office in America. **Hardly had I entered** the building when Bill Gates greeted me in the entrance hall.
I've been working for him for two years now and **not for a minute have I regretted** that decision. **Never have I had** a more interesting time in my life.

11
1. **Do sit down,** please.
2. I **did put** them away this morning.
3. **Do be** quiet, please.
4. We **did enjoy** every minute.

12
1. No, grandma, it's Jeff (who) I'm going out with.
2. No, it was at a school concert that I met him.
3. No, it's a party (that) we are going to. / It's to a party that we're going.
4. Sally: No, it is Jo (who) she's going out with.

13
1. Carl repaired the computer **himself**.
2. They say so **themselves**.
3. That **itself** is too difficult for many people.
4. But we found a solution **ourselves**.
5. She had written the computer programme **herself**.
6. I always download software **myself**.

14
1. A(n) **really / very / extremely / quite** strange film was made in the old castle.
2. One of the actors was a **terribly / very / really** old man.
3. Making the film was **extremely / very / quite / really** difficult.
4. In the end, the film was **quite / very / extremely / really** well produced.
5. The crew had done a(n) **very / really / extremely** good job.

15
1. What we all need are holidays.
2. What Sarah told us was very interesting.
3. What my dad did was turn off the computer.
4. What James does is very dangerous.

16
1. I **play** / ~~am playing~~ in the school football team.
2. We ~~play~~ / **are playing** well this season.
3. Sue ~~does~~ / **is doing** her homework at the moment.
4. Luke **does** / ~~is doing~~ his homework regularly.
5. Listen, Jeff ~~plays~~ / **is playing** the trumpet again!
6. Sorry, nobody ~~works~~ / **is working** today.
7. My sister **doesn't work** / ~~isn't working~~ as a teacher.
8. The earth **moves** / ~~is moving~~ around the sun.

17
1. I **bought** a very interesting book yesterday.
2. Jake **has spent** the last of his money.
3. The USA **became** independent in 1776.
4. I **have seen** this movie twice so far.
5. When **did** you **come** home last night?
6. I **spoke** to Mr Taylor five minutes ago.
7. Megan **hasn't been** to Germany yet.
8. We **ate** an awful pizza for lunch today.

18
1. Tracy and Jean **have been playing** the guitar **for** two hours.
2. Rob **has been waiting** for his girlfriend **for** twenty minutes.
3. They **have been running** through the park **since** 9 o'clock this morning.
4. Dad **has been reading** the newspaper **since** he came home from work.
5. This shop **has been selling** tea **for** more than 150 years.
6. Mr Clark **has been riding** his bike to work **since** he crashed his car.

19

Old Mrs Greedy:	I **was checking** on the maids.
The maids:	We **were cleaning** the rooms downstairs.
Tina and Tony:	We **were playing** in our room. But we saw our grandma when she **was walking** along the corridor.
Mr Green:	I **was cutting** down the old tree. I saw Mrs Greedy. She **was talking** very loudly to Mr Neverenoughmoney.
Mr Nolimit:	I **was repairing** the old Bentley in the garage when I heard the shot.

20
1. On the day of the Hardys' move, it **started** to rain while they **were carrying** their furniture to the street in front of their house.
2. But the big lorry which they **needed wasn't** there.
3. Everything **got / was getting** wet while they **were waiting**.
4. When the lorry finally **arrived** they first **put** the sofa inside.
5. While they **were still carrying** their furniture outside the lorry driver suddenly **drove** away with most of their things.
6. Since then the Hardys **have been living** without most of their furniture.
7. The police **have been trying** to find the driver but they **haven't been** successful yet.
8. As the insurance company **hasn't paid** any money yet, the Hardys **have got** used to living without a sofa and chairs.

21
My grandfather **was** born in a small village in Jamaica in 1929. He **left** school when he **was** 14 years old. He **had already worked** in a few different jobs when he **decided** to go to Britain. He **had saved** some money, so he **bought** a ticket for a ship to England.
When he **arrived** in London he **realized** that someone **had stolen** most of his money. He **got** a job as a dishwasher in a restaurant, but he only

stayed there for a few months. However, he **didn't like** his second job at the London harbour any better. This **wasn't** what he **had left** Jamaica for. But in his new job he **met** a lot of other immigrants from the Caribbean. None of them **liked** the food in England. They **missed** their traditional food. My grandpa **remembered** that his mother **had taught** him a lot of recipes. So he **opened** one of the first Caribbean restaurants in London.

22
1. He **had been waiting** for his girlfriend for more than half an hour.
2. They **had been shopping** the whole afternoon.
3. She **had been thinking** about her boyfriend all day.
4. He **had been painting** the kitchen for five hours.
5. She **had been studying** for her exams since lunchtime.

23 TV **became** popular in the 1950s. In Britain, for example, a lot of people **bought** their first TV sets to watch how Elizabeth **became** queen in 1953. As the importance of television **grew**, more and more programmes **appeared.** Suddenly people **could / were able to** watch the news. Before, they **had just listened** to them on the radio or **(had) read** the newspapers.
Since the 1960s more and more entertainment programmes such as soap operas **have appeared / have been appearing** on television. At first they **showed** a world in which everybody **lived** a happy life, so that people **could / were able to dream** while they **were watching** the programme. But after some time the soaps **started** to show more realistic situations. "East Enders", which **is** one of the most important British soap operas today, **is** set in London's East End and **shows** all the problems of the people who **live** there.
This trend **has continued / has been continuing** in the new millennium and recently reality shows **have become** a big success. Almost every channel **produces** its own reality show. As these programmes **are** often interrupted by commercials, they **are** a big market for the advertising industry too. So viewers who **watch** the shows **don't always enjoy** them.

24
1. I saw my English teacher in town yesterday.
2. We have been living in this house for ten years.
3. After I had bought a new mobile, I sold my old one.
4. Josh was (just) walking down the street when a reporter asked him some questions.
5. The Jacksons have gone shopping. There is nobody at home.

25 victim – somebody who has been / is attacked
refuge – safe place which offers protection from somebody or something
to remove – to get rid of something
culprit – a person who has done something wrong
humiliation – an act which makes somebody feel a sense of shame
to commit suicide – to kill oneself
to manipulate – to change something, to make somebody act the way you want
to blame – to say or think that somebody has done something wrong

26 1. false; 2. false; 3. true; 4. true; 5. false; 6. false

27 Der Text ist brauchbar.
Gründe *(beispielhaft)*: Er bietet einen kurzen Überblick. Er berücksichtigt (fast) alle modernen Medien. Er ist gut verständlich.

28 British teenagers use their mobiles to: send text messages, exchange photos and videos, download pictures or short films from the Internet, surf the Internet, talk to other people (not a lot).

8

Dialogue 1

Boy: Let's see what's on at the cinema tonight. Oh cool, the new Tarantino film!
Girl: Oh no, not another action film! There's always so much shooting and shouting, explosions and stuff. It's Friday night and I just want to chill after this week. What about "Vampire Lovebites"? The actor who's playing the main role is just so cute.
Boy: No way, I hate him! And anyway, school's so boring all week. I need some proper action. And you get that from Tarantino, he's just one of the best directors ever. He even got an Oscar for this film.
Girl: Maybe, but is there even any kind of story or plot? I've read the book "Vampire Lovebites" and the story is pretty awesome, so romantic, especially when …
Boy: Okay, okay, okay, you really don't have to tell me. But this action film has got a historical background, so even you might enjoy it. And don't forget: It's funny too.

Dialogue 2

Boy: Have you had a look at the programme yet?
Girl: Well, actually, there's this fantasy film I thought we could go and see.
Boy: Oh come on, you know exactly what I think of fantasy films. They're so – well – unreal.

Girl: Don't take the story so seriously. If you ignore the weird stuff and just enjoy the great pictures, the shots of the countryside and the close-ups of old buildings it's a really great film. I know you like history and this is definitely a film for history lovers.

Boy: Yeah, I do like history, but that means real history, something that really happened. Just like that other film – you remember the one about the American President during the American Civil War? Something like that gives you real information. It'd be good for you, too. Remember we're starting that project about the Civil War at school next week.

Girl: Hm, Civil War sounds like action, that's true. But the people in these historical dramas usually just talk all the time. I like films with action, and that's exactly what you get in this fantasy film. And it's even in 3D ! But then … maybe you're right. Perhaps I should do something for my History mark. Let's watch the historical drama. But it had better help me with that school project ! And then you can get me a fantasy film on DVD … seeing as it's my birthday next month !

Dialogue 3

Boy: This week was so horrible, I really need a good laugh now – any comedy would be fine. I don't even care what the story is. It's just got to be funny.

Girl: Sorry, but that's not exactly what I had in mind. I was thinking something … a bit different.

Boy: Different – like what?

Girl: Well, for example something really unusual, something you don't see in cinemas all the time.

Boy: You aren't talking about that musical, are you?

Girl: Yeah, exactly !

Boy: You can't be serious ! They just sing all the time ! You can't understand a word and if there are funny scenes, you almost certainly miss them because of all the music going on.

Girl: Sorry, not true. There are subtitles, you know, so you could just read them if you have problems understanding the actors. You'll get into the plot very quickly too because the story is really interesting. Besides, the music won't kill you !

Boy: Okay, you've convinced me. But don't get mad if I laugh in all the wrong places.

29 **Dialogue 1**

Boy: action film
Reasons: good action, good director, Oscar, historical background, funny parts

Girl: romance
Reasons: cute actor, great story / plot

Dialogue 2

Girl: fantasy film
Reasons: great camera shots, nice scenery, for history lovers, action, *3D*

Boy: historical drama
Reasons: real history / information, helpful for school project

Dialogue 3

Boy: comedy
Reasons: good laugh, funny

Girl: musical
Reasons: something different, subtitles, interesting story

9

Talk show host: Good afternoon, ladies and gentlemen. Welcome to our show "No sorry, that's not true." Today we're going to talk about modern media in our everyday life. The show promises to be very interesting as we have two guests with quite different opinions on this topic.
Mrs Jane McEwan, Member of Parliament for the Conservative Party and spokeswoman for education, and Mr Marc Douglas-Ford of the newly founded Orange Party, which supports a more open and freer use of modern media, especially the Internet.
Mrs McEwan, in an interview last week, you spoke strongly for the regulation of the Internet. Could you repeat your main points again, please?

McEwan: Yes, of course. But first I must make it clear that I am not against the Internet as such. I think it offers fantastic opportunities for communication and research, but we mustn't forget the problems and even dangers that it brings.
First of all, we have the duty to protect our children and teenagers. Only think of all the negative influences like violence or pornography on the Internet. Or the websites where racists make their opinions public.

It's not easy for young people to filter the information they find on the Internet. They can be easily influenced by one-dimensional arguments.
And finally, there is a growing number of criminals who use the Internet. They pose dangers not only for the economy, but also for everyone who uses the Internet and has to give personal details like credit card numbers.
So, as I said before, the Internet has become important. We can't live without it, but as it plays such an important role in our everyday life, there have to be some regulations to make it safe.

Talk show host: I see. Thanks for that. Now Mr Douglas-Ford, this is not what you and your party are campaigning for, is it?

Douglas-Ford: Yes, you are right. But I must say that I agree with Mrs McEwan on one point: young people mustn't have access to pornography, racism or violence. But I think a lot is done by Internet providers to limit access to these sites.
You have a point when you mention the growing number of criminals using the Internet. But if we take a closer look at your example regarding credit card numbers: all the big and well-known banks are doing everything to protect their customers. It's in their own interest to make Internet banking safe. And don't forget, more and more products are sold via the Internet. So it's in the interest of these companies too to guarantee safe payment.
Finally, if you want to control and regulate the Internet, who is going to control the controllers? We still live in a free country where everybody can say or write what they want. This has always been an important issue in our society. With a free and unregulated world wide web we can support the people who live in undemocratic societies like China by offering them unfiltered and uncensored information about their own country.
Besides, if you really want to control and regulate the Internet, you can't do it in just one country. You'd need all the countries in the world to cooperate as the Internet connects people worldwide.

McEwan: Yes, but I see a problem for our culture. Fewer books are sold and quite a few newspapers have problems or aren't printed anymore. As a consequence, we lose our great variety of opinions because only a few newspapers will survive and they will be controlled by one or two big companies.

Douglas-Ford: I'm sorry, Mrs McEwan, but your argument can't convince me. Newspapers use the Internet themselves. They even advertise online for their websites. So, even if some of the newspapers no longer appear in a printed version, there's still a great variety of them online. And by the way, the news on the Internet is always more up-to-date than the news in the newspapers, because it's being updated constantly. You can download newspaper apps onto your mobile or tablet so that you have access to more information than you can buy at the newsagent's. And don't forget the information you can find on blogs, twitter or on social networking sites. More and more celebrities, politicians and political organisations use these modern ways of communication.

McEwan: Oh yes, everybody has an opinion on everything these days. And this is exactly one of the reasons why young people are almost addicted to their mobiles. Young people can do almost everything with them, and they do nothing else. And the problem is that teenagers especially don't think about the dangers when they spend hour after hour on social networking sites. Of course I know that these sites play an important role in their lives, but kids are too careless. They put personal things online, which often makes them targets for bullying. There have even been cases of teenagers killing themselves as a result.

Douglas-Ford: Oh no, you can't be serious. I admit that there have been such terrible reactions to cyberbullying. But when you look at the number of people who use these social networking sites every day, you won't be able to express these cases in percent. You should rather think of all the positive aspects of these sites. They're used as the modern way of getting in contact with other people and of exchanging all kinds of information.
After all, social networking sites aren't only used by young people but also by adults, by people like you and me, and even by big companies. Let me give you one example of the use of modern media today. A pupil who's missed school can be easily informed about homework by a classmate on a social networking site.

Talk show host: I'm awfully sorry to interrupt this discussion, but our time is up. I want to thank you both for this interesting discussion.

30

Pro	Con
– way of communication and research – using the Internet, e.g. for payment, is made safe by banks and online shops – a lot of products are sold on the Internet – way to share news and information – modern and quick way to get information or news – a lot of people use modern media – means of offering people in China, for example, unfiltered information about their country	– negative influence, e.g. violence, pornography or racism – filtering information is difficult – users can be influenced – criminals use the internet – danger for printed media and variety of opinion

31 *Musterlösung*

1. She uses different kinds of oil for her body and hair.
2. She's going to wear light clothes in bright colours.
3. She's going to spend her holidays in the Black Forest.
4. She loves the nature there.
5. She doesn't say anything about that.

32 *Musterlösung*

Hi everybody
Of course, mobiles are very important for us. But Janice, do you really think that you need your mobile all the time? You are right when you write about all the positive aspects, but I think the mobile can distract you when you use it during lessons. But I also think that we should be allowed to use the mobile during break time.

Das sollte in deiner Lösung enthalten sein:

☐ Du nimmst Bezug auf einige der bisher angesprochenen Argumente.

☐ Du äußerst deine eigene Meinung und begründest sie.

Mögliche Pro-Argumente:
– you need mobiles for research
– you need them to call your parents
– you can contact friends when they are ill (homework, etc.)

Mögliche Contra-Argumente:
– mobiles distract during lessons (calls, games)
– they are used for illegal recording of other people
– they are used for taking photos or making videos illegally
– they are used for cheating in tests

Revision B

1

1. Most young people use electronic **media / equipment** today.
2. There is no definite **opinion / rule** about how much pocket money should be given.
3. There are **regulations / laws** that regulate when young people can get an official job.
4. **Parents** should set a good example in financial issues.
5. The biggest financial **problem / issue** for young people today is their mobile phone bill.

10

Tour guide: Good morning, ladies and gentlemen, and welcome to our tour of the Neustadt Studios. First, let me give you some basic facts about the studios and their history.
Our studios cover an area of about half a square kilometre. This includes the indoor studios, the outdoor areas for filming and of course our offices. Unfortunately, we won't be able to visit everything, as some areas are being used at the moment. But hopefully you'll get a good impression of our studios and the many different aspects of making a film.
At the moment, about 6,000 people work here at the studios. Most of them belong to the film crews, like sound technicians, cameramen and women or electricians. But there are also lots of other people on the staff: people like me who show tourists around or the cooks and waiters at the cafeteria.

Visitor: Are there any famous actors or actresses here at the moment?

Tour guide: Well, it depends on what you call famous. We don't get celebrities like George Clooney or Angelina Jolie very often, I'm afraid. They mainly work in Hollywood. But if you think of German actors and actresses, you might get a chance to see and perhaps even meet some of them. Additionally, there are all the people who work as extras or have minor roles.

Visitor: Excuse me, what do you have to do to become an extra?

Tour guide: The roles for extras used to be advertised in the local newspapers. Nowadays you just have to check our website.

If you're lucky, you can get such a part.
Five to ten big films are produced here every year. Our studios also produce about 30 to 40 commercials for cinemas and television.
Our studio was founded in 1924, in the golden age of silent films. But the actors and actresses had to learn talking quickly, as films with sound replaced the silent films.
The studios have been in permanent use since the 1920s, although there have been some ups and downs over the years.
Before we start our tour, I'd just like to remind everyone that you're not allowed to take photos or record anything. And make sure that your mobiles are turned off. Thank you.
Okay, ladies and gentlemen, if you'd like to follow me, please. …
… We're now standing in front of our second-largest studio. A new episode of the detective series "Polizei ermittelt" is being produced here at the moment. Normally, we wouldn't be allowed to take a look inside, but we're lucky, the team is away on location today.

Visitor: Do you know where they are and what they are doing?

Tour guide: I'm sorry, I don't know. And even if I knew, I wouldn't be allowed to tell you. They don't want anybody to know before the film or the episode is first shown on TV.
So please, when we go in there, don't touch anything and be careful, there might be cables on the floor. …
… The part of our studios that we're now coming to is the most modern one. The studios here are mainly used for making commercials. Although many scenes are animated with the help of computers, there are still real people acting in commercials.

Visitor: If it's possible to make commercials with computer software, why don't you always do it? I mean, wouldn't the production be cheaper because you wouldn't have to pay so many people?

Tour guide: Actually, no. Creating animated commercials is still more expensive than producing commercials with a small number of actors. And on the other hand I think customers want to see real people when they're being told to buy a certain kind of cheese or to bring their money to a bank.
Now, a good commercial needs good music too, and this is what's happening in the building over there. …
… Ladies and gentlemen, we've almost reached the end of our tour. We're standing in front of the oldest part of our studios. Everything started in this building here.

The old studios were used until the late 1960s, but by then they had become too small and the equipment was really old-fashioned. After the new studios had been built, the old rooms were used to store the old equipment used for films. About ten years ago, the whole building was turned into our visitor centre, as visitor numbers have continually risen every year.
Please take a look inside. You can buy old film posters or old equipment from films or series. Just walk around. You can still feel the atmosphere. Or just sit and relax in the café with a nice piece of cake and a cup of coffee.
I'd like to take this opportunity to thank you for your visit and your interest in Neustadt Studios. Good-bye and have a safe trip home.

2

1. The tour guide ~~**can**~~ **/ cannot** show all areas of the studio.
2. There **are /** ~~**aren't**~~ people on the staff who don't have anything to do with film making.
3. It **is possible /** ~~**is not possible**~~ to get a role as an extra.
4. Visitors ~~**are**~~ **/ aren't** allowed to use their mobiles during the tour.
5. The films **are /** ~~**aren't**~~ kept secret.
6. Computers **are /** ~~**aren't**~~ used for the production of commercials.
7. The visitor centre **offers /** ~~**doesn't offer**~~ a lot of things.

3 *Musterlösung:*

I'm back from my summer holidays and I must tell you about the most interesting thing I did during my holidays. My parents and I visited the oldest film studios in Germany.
Most of the popular TV series and programmes are produced there, plus almost all the commercials you can see on TV. And guess what! I saw this good-looking guy from this shampoo commercial. Unfortunately I wasn't able to talk to him or ask him for an autograph. I must try to get a job as an extra. Maybe I could then act in a commercial with him. That would be awesome.
Then we were allowed to have a look into one of the studios where they were filming a popular German detective series.
The visitor centre was fantastic, too. My parents went almost crazy when they saw all the old film posters there. And by the way, they serve the best apple pie!
Unfortunately, I can't offer any pictures as we were not allowed to take photos.

Das sollte in deiner Lösung enthalten sein:

- ☐ Du nimmst einige der Informationen aus dem Hörtext auf.
- ☐ Du schreibst darüber wie über eigene Erfahrungen (in der Ich-Form) und malst dir die Situation weiter aus.
- ☐ Du berichtest, was dir gefallen und was dir nicht gefallen hat, und gibst eigene Ansichten wider.

4 Wir dürfen die Bilder nicht einfach einscannen und ins Netz stellen. Das verstößt gegen das Copyright. Wenn wir dagegen verstoßen, kann es sehr teuer werden, da die Unterhaltungsfirmen, welche die Rechte an bekannten (Comic-)Figuren haben, streng gegen Copyrightverletzungen vorgehen. Wir müssen bei jedem Bild die Copyrightregelung beachten. Das gilt auch für die Soundfiles.

Unit 4

1

1. **Child labour** is still **tolerated** in some **developing countries**.
2. A **dictator** can't rule without a **secret police**.
3. **In spite of equal opportunities,** the situation of women is not **satisfactory**.
4. The **dignity** of **lesbians** and **gays** is often not respected.
5. **Courage** was the only **appropriate** way to end **racial segregation**.
6. The **concept** of **slavery** was **common** in all societies of the **ancient** world.
7. The **parliament passed** the **necessary law** against **everyday racism**.
8. Your **double standards** are **obnoxious** and you **offend** other people.

2

R						S					T			
U		P	E	A	C	E	F	U	L		E			
M						G					R			
O	R	D	I	N	A	R	Y				R			
R						E		A	N	C	I	E	N	T
						G					F			
					H	A	R	M	O	N	I	O	U	S
						T					E			L
M		D		T	H	I	C	K			D			A
A		E				O				S				V
L	E	A	S	T		N		P	R	I	V	A	T	E
E		T								L				R
		H								E				Y
										N				
							W	E	S	T	E	R	N	

3

1. I **received** a nice letter yesterday.
2. It took very long to pass this **act**.
3. If you don't study, you won't get good **marks**.
4. Rose was **terrified** when she heard the news.
5. The politician was **murdered** in bright daylight.
6. Traffic is a **common** problem in most big cities.
7. This ring is of great **worth** to me.
8. I can't **handle** his strange ideas.

4

1. to free: animals, slaves
2. to recruit: a soldier, an activist
3. to spread: butter, a rumor
4. to vote for: a woman, a song
5. to receive: a present, a postcard
6. to pass: a law, the station

5

Die Sätze sind lediglich Beispiele für mögliche Lösungen.
1. **authoritarian regime:** The people demonstrated against the authoritarian regime.
2. **exotic ingredient:** We are using exotic ingredients for this meal.
3. **realistic concept:** The new boss has a realistic concept for the company.
4. **curious child:** A curious child learns a lot.
5. **peaceful activist:** A peaceful activist was arrested by the police.

6

1. Our team qualified **for** the next round.
2. Tracy has spread nasty rumors **about** her last boyfriend.
3. I can't identify **with** the characters in that book.
4. My mum complained **about** the service in the hotel.
5. My grandfather always spoke **out** against racism.
6. I don't know who to vote **for**.
7. You can't judge people **by** their clothes.
8. My dad has always been a role model **for** me.
9. There are a lot of references **to** politics in this song.

7

Verb	Noun	Adjective
tolerate	tolerance	tolerant
free	freedom	free
respect	respect	respectful
die	death	dead

1. We need more **tolerance** in our society.
2. We should **tolerate** other cultures more.
3. The fight for **freedom** has always been an important issue.
4. Only **free** people can live together peacefully.
5. A **respectful** way of living together is very important.
6. Only if we show **respect** to others can we expect the same from them.
7. People who **die** while fighting for a religious cause have a very special status in some societies.
8. For them **death** doesn't mean the end.

8

1. **The rich** often live in separated areas.
2. There are a lot of **rich** people in this club.
3. A lot of **old** people live alone.
4. **The old** might become a problem for younger generations.
5. A **poor** man is begging for money.
6. The government doesn't do enough for **the poor**.

9

Positive	Neutral	Negative
amazing	ambitious	aggressive
attractive	average	angry
awesome	bald	authoritarian
beautiful		awful
brave		boring
clever		cold
confident		

10

Hi everybody. My name is Amy Donald. I love **reading**. I'm a big fan of Harry Potter. I love **watching** the films too, and I'm dreaming of **visiting** the places where the films were made. I also enjoy **riding** my bike. Actually, I prefer **riding** the bike to **walking** and I also don't like **taking** the bus because I hate **standing** in a crowded bus.
I enjoy **spending** time with friends. I love **meeting** people and **making** new friends. I play two instruments, but I prefer **playing** the guitar to **practicing** the piano.
Now I hope you don't mind me **talking** so much. I'm looking forward to **getting** to know you all.

11

1. This government is really **bad at ruling** the country.
2. Those politicians are only **famous for raising** taxes.
3. They are just **keen on staying** in power.
4. They are not interested **in listening to** the people.
5. We have got **used to living** with useless politicians.

12

1. The activists had the chance of visiting the sweatshop.
2. They were furious about seeing children at work.
3. The workers were afraid of talking to the activists.
4. But the activists were used to interviewing such people.

13

1 E When Gandhi lived in South Africa, he worked as a lawyer in spite of **not being** white.
2 D He fought for the rights of Indians in South Africa without **protesting** against the discrimination against black South Africans, too.
3 F But then he moved to India instead of **staying** in South Africa.
4 I In India he informed himself of the people's problems by **travelling** through the country.
5 J He thought of new ways to protest apart from **just writing** letters to politicians.
6 A But instead of **fighting** with weapons he chose non-violent forms of protest.
7 C He continued his actions in spite of **being** sent to prison a few times.
8 G More and more people supported him by **joining** his actions.
9 H Finally the British gave India its independence instead of **continuing** the fight.
10 B In the end, Gandhi was killed in spite of **being** considered the hero of Indian independence.

14

1. It is important for everybody to accept other opinions.
2. It is not always easy for parents to listen to their teenage children.
3. There are strict rules for the media to follow.
4. It is sometimes hard for politicians to say the truth.
5. It is wrong for shops to sell dangerous toys.
6. There are laws for employers to provide women with equal job opportunities.
7. It is dangerous for governments not to listen to the people.

15

1. I don't know **how to carry** the sign.
2. I have no idea **what to say** if a reporter asks me questions.
3. I don't know **where to go** after the demonstration.
4. I don't know **who / whom to ask** if there is a problem.

16

Hi I'm Peggy. I want **to** leave school as soon as possible, but my parents won't let me do it. They expect me **to** go to university. But I would prefer **to** do on-the-job training, perhaps as a car mechanic. I would like **to** join an organisation which helps in developing countries so that I could help the people there. But it seems **to** be difficult for my parents **to** accept my plan. They don't want me **to** leave school. They say that if I really wish **to** help other people, I should also finish school first. Then I would have the chance **to** study. And after that it might be easier for me **to** decide what **to** do. It is their dream **to** see their daughter at university. I would be the first in our family **to** study.

17 1. I heard a police car **speed** up the road.
2. I saw those kids **play** football on the fresh grass.
3. I felt my feet **get** wet in the rain.

18 I'll always remember **living** as a slave all those years ago. We started **to work / working** very early. We weren't allowed to stop **to have** a short break on very hot days. Sometimes it felt like **being** in hell. But we had to continue **to collect / collecting** cotton till we had our lunch break. We were looking forward to **hearing** the command to stop **working**. Then we began **to walk / walking** to our small houses. At night, we often dreamed about **running** away. I'll never forget **seeing** the soldiers of the North, who were fighting for our liberty. It meant **being** free at last.

19 1. Children **can / are allowed to / may** play here.
2. You **can't / are not able to / may not** visit the museum today.
3. You **can't / mustn't / are not allowed to** use this door.
4. You **may / can** get tickets there.
5. You **mustn't / are not allowed to / can't** take the dog inside. / You **must** leave the dog outside. / Dogs **mustn't / are not allowed to** go here.
6. You **may / can / are allowed to / should** park the car there.
7. You **should / must / have to** be careful when you go swimming.
8. You **can / may / should** get information there.

20 1. John told me (that) he was going to help his father paint the kitchen.
2. Megan explained (that) she had gone to bed late the day before so she was too tired to run the race.
3. Terry answered (that) he wouldn't have time because his cousin was coming.
4. Dan said (that) he was sorry, but a friend had invited him to his house.

21 1. The secretary told me to wait outside.
2. The head teacher asked me to find my classroom on my own.
3. A classmate told me not to sit there, but to sit next to Amy.
4. A teacher wanted me not to leave my books on my desk but to put them into my locker.

22 1. A reporter asked if / whether he had already met the Queen.
2. He wanted to know what the future would bring for our country.
3. He asked him why he hadn't spoken out against racism.
4. He wanted to know when he was going to fly to Germany.
5. He asked if / whether he believed that Scotland would become independent.

23 My dad wanted to know what I was going to do last night.
I asked him if / whether I hadn't told him about the protest march. I explained they wanted to close down our youth club.
My father replied that he didn't want me to go to a protest march when I hadn't finished my homework.
I told him I could do it the next day / the following day. I added that that march was really important for me and that Tom and Chris were coming, too.
My dad told me to stop talking about those boys. He pointed out that he didn't care about them. Then he wanted to know if / whether I didn't remember what I had promised mum and him after I had shown them my school report last year.
I admitted that he was right. I argued I had been studying all day and I would do my homework today. I told him to let me go and I explained that it was really important that a lot of people came to that protest march. Then I asked him if / whether he hadn't gone to the same youth club when he had been young.
He said I might go but that I had to do my homework today. Finally he wanted to know when I would be back and asked me not to come too late. I thanked him and told him he was the best. I promised him I wouldn't be late.

24 C What is the problem?
A What is the situation?
D What might the future hold?
B What do the United Nations want?

25
1. The right to clean drinking water is an important issue which has been formally accepted by **the UN and UNESCO**.
2. Clean drinking water is important because **people need it for their personal and daily use like washing or cooking.**
3. Developing countries are supported by the WHO with **help and advice**.
4. When people have to carry their water from sources that are kilometres away it means that **they can only use a little water per day**.
5. For people living in the big cities of developing countries the **high prices** for water are a big problem.
6. In the future, people who don't have access to enough drinking water might **fight for it** or **work together**.

11

Demonstration 1

"This government makes me sick. How can this tyrant think even for a moment that we would believe those numbers? He doesn't believe himself that more than two thirds of the people voted for him and his gang of criminals! Ask around, travel round the country and you'll meet more people against him than people who do support him and his politics.
Do you see that group of men wearing the black coats? His secret police! They're the only reason why he's still in power. But this has to end. We want free elections so that we can live in a free country."

Demonstration 2

"Have you seen the pictures taken in that factory? They show children as young as six or eight working in a sweatshop. Don't they have human rights like adults? How can they have a future when they aren't allowed to go to school and get an education?
But it's not just a problem in developing countries. We, the buyers in rich countries, are part of it too. As long as we don't want to pay fair prices, these children will work in slave-like conditions. We must be prepared to pay what the products are worth. We must convince stores and shops to sell fairly priced clothes so that the situation for these poor children can change and they can go to school instead of having to work."

Demonstration 3

"Well, I agree, a lot has changed in recent years. At least we don't have to ask our husbands if we're allowed to work and earn our own money. But there's still room for improvement. On the one hand politicians want more women to go to university, but on the other hand the same politicians with their dated opinions make it almost impossible for women to get good and high-paid jobs. Look at the bosses and managers of all those big companies. Most of them are men. How many women can you name who are in top management positions? Even today it's still very difficult for women with children to be successful in their careers and make it to the top. And as long as there are men in power who think women are less suitable as top managers, women will not have equal opportunities."

Demonstration 4

"I'm really not a communist, but we can't go on like this. There are more and more people living in poverty in our country. And it's a scandal that although most of these people do work they don't earn enough to support their family. And then look at managers and bankers: the money they get increases year after year. But our politicians are afraid of them. Some of them might even work for the big bosses. That's the only explanation why those millionaires don't give their fair share to support our society. If they had to give a share of their wealth to the state, they wouldn't have to change their standard of living, but the poor could be supported much better."

26 1. **2**; 2. **4**; 3. **1**; 4. **3**; 5. **2**; 6. **4**; 7. **2**; 8. **1**; 9. **3**

12

Dave: Hi Ben. What's up?
Ben: Hi Dave. Have you already had a look at the new school rules?
Dave: Well, I skimmed through them, but I couldn't find anything new. I've got it here. Look, that's it. We must be in the classrooms as soon as the bell has rung.
Ben: Yeah, but nobody is in the classrooms after the bell has rung. We're always hanging around in the corridors till the teachers come. Are there any changes about mobile phones?
Dave: We're still not allowed to use mobile phones at school, not even in the breaks. Oh, and look, bad news for you. In the future, we won't be allowed to bring any other electronic things, like iPods, iPads or computer games to school.
Ben: No way! No iPod, no games, how am I supposed to survive the long breaks, especially lunch break?
Dave: Oh, talking about breaks, there is another new rule. "All students must leave the classrooms during breaks."
Ben: That's okay in summer or when the weather is good. But what about in winter or bad weather? Can you imagine all of us standing in our small entrance hall when everybody has to leave the classroom? That's sure to cause problems.
Dave: Yeah, you're right. Think of that group of bullies who are always after the younger kids, although there has always been the rule that we should be tolerant and respectful towards everybody here at school.
Ben: I don't think that the Shaw brothers and their gang of bullies have ever heard words like tolerance and respect and I don't think they even know what these words mean.
Dave: True. But they might get into real trouble with the head teacher now.
Ben: Why? They've got away with almost everything. They're always late.
Dave: That's the point. In the future, the doors will be locked after the bell has rung. So everybody who's late has to use the main entrance, which means they have to pass the head's office. And you know how strict she is about being late.

27

New	Old
Leave the classroom during breaks.	Be in the classroom when the bell has rung.
No other electronic equipment (iPod, computer games) is allowed.	No mobile phones are allowed.
Doors will be locked when lessons have begun.	Be tolerant and respectful towards everybody.

13

Talk show host: Hallo, ladies and gentlemen, and welcome to our programme "History at lunchtime". Today my guest is Professor Thomas Williamson from the University of Newcastle and we'll be talking about the history of human rights. Professor Williamson, the year 2015 will mark the 800th birthday of the Magna Carta. So, a document from the Middle Ages – does that really have any importance for us today?

Williamson: Well, from our modern point of view that might seem a good question. But let's take a look at the early 13th century first, shall we? For people living in 1215, the Magna Carta meant a great change, something unheard of before. Suddenly, their king was forced to sign a document that guaranteed certain rights to noblemen like barons or dukes. He also had to state that the law was more important than his personal will. Of course, for most of the normal people nothing much changed in their everyday lives. But at least they could now be sure that the king couldn't have them hanged just because he didn't like their nose or, more important, because he wanted their land. And that is exactly the reason why the Magna Carta is still important today: We rightly consider it the starting point of some of our ideas of democracy, individual rights and personal freedom.

Talk show host: But our ancestors in the Middle Ages hadn't themselves invented the idea of giving rights to the people, had they?

Williamson: You've got a point there. The idea that a person has certain rights can already be found in the works of philosophers like Plato, Aristotle or Cicero in ancient Greece and Rome. However, in those societies the word *person* meant only a small part of the population: only men, and only such men who were born free. The same is true for the time of the Magna Carta.

Talk show host: But that seems far away. When we think of human rights today, we're more likely to look back no more than 250 years, to the American Declaration of Independence of 1776 and the French Revolution of 1789.

Williamson: Yes, of course. But ideas of human rights had been introduced by philosophers of the 17th and 18th century. The colonists in America were the first to turn them into political action when they declared the colonies independent. They argued that they were in the right by declaring that "all men are created equal and have certain rights like life or liberty". But a closer look shows that again only a small part of the population was meant. People who owned less than a certain amount of money, Native Americans, the great number of black slaves in the southern colonies and of course women didn't have those rights.

Talk show host: So what changed in the French Revolution?

Williamson: Well, basically the French Revolution brought the first written list of human and civil rights. But these idealistic thoughts were soon forgotten when the revolution grew more and more radical. As a consequence, the whole idea of liberty and equality turned into a tyranny. And the problem with every kind of tyranny is that the people lose their rights.

Talk show host: So when did human rights become a reality for everyone, at least here in the Western world?

Williamson: Well, it's not easy to give an exact date or year, but the development began in the 19th century when workers fought for their dignity and rights. Then at the beginning of the 20th century, women campaigned for the right to vote, which might be considered the most important of all civil rights. But it was World War II which brought the breakthrough. From the American point of view, the war with Nazi Germany was a battle for democracy and human rights against Fascism. Shortly after the end of the war, the USA was the driving force behind the declaration of human rights by the United Nations. Since then, more and more countries have accepted this catalogue of human rights.

Talk show host: Could you answer one last question: What does the future hold for human rights?

Williamson: Uh, that's a difficult one. Human and civil rights are now widely accepted throughout the world. But the fight for them must continue as long as there are regimes that don't want to give human and civil rights to their people.

Talk show host: Thank you, Professor Williamson.

28 1. true; 2. false; 3. false; 4. true; 5. false; 6. true; 7. true; 8. false; 9. true

29 *Musterlösung:*

Georg Elser: A quiet hero
Georg Elser was born in Hermaringen in Württemberg in 1903 as the son of working class parents. In the 1920s Georg Elser learnt different jobs, and he was good with his hands. After some years away from home, he returned to his hometown in 1932. There he worked on his parents' farm and in a factory which produced things needed for the war.
He was quiet and didn't have many close friends. On the one hand he was very religious, but on the other hand he was active in a Socialist organisation.
Georg Elser realized that the Nazi government was preparing for war. As he always followed his own ideas, he decided to act and to kill the tyrant Hitler. Being clever and good with his hands, he built a bomb on his own and hid it in the Bürgerbräukeller in Munich where Hitler was expected to hold a speech on 8th November 1939. The perfectly made bomb exploded at exactly the planned time that evening, but Hitler had already left the building a few minutes earlier.
The same night, Georg Elser was caught by the police. He was murdered in the KZ Dachau on 9th April 1945, one month before the Second World War ended and the Nazi regime was over.

Das sollte in deiner Lösung enthalten sein:

- ☐ Du hast den Text chronologisch aufgebaut.
- ☐ Du hast die Daten aus dem Lebenslauf verwendet.
- ☐ Du erklärst Elsers Gründe für den Anschlag (active in a socialist organization, realized that Hitler was preparing for war).
- ☐ Du hast Charaktereigenschaften aufgenommen (quiet, not many friends, religious, followed his own ideas, clever, intelligent, clever with his hands) und in den Text verarbeitet, sodass deutlich wird, warum und wie Elser den Anschlag geplant hat.
- ☐ Du hast Informationen weggelassen, die in diesem Zusammenhang weniger wichtig sind (helped repair the church tower, question if he went to church regularly, excitement in town after Elser's arrest, liked nature and went for walks, question if he had had a helper).
- ☐ Du hast eine Überschrift gewählt, die etwas über Elsers Bedeutung aussagt.

30 Rachel hat die späten 1960er im Geschichtsunterricht durchgenommen. Sie möchte gerne etwas über die Zeit in Deutschland erfahren.
It was an exciting and interesting time here, too. Although grandfather wasn't in Berlin, i.e. in the centre of the action, there was lots going on where he lived, too.
In Amerika protestierten die Leute gegen den Vietnamkrieg und Rassentrennung. Und bei uns?
The war in Vietnam was important, too, but the conflict between generations was even more important. Young people wanted to know what their fathers had done during the Nazi regime as no one ever talked about that time.
Wie wichtig war Politik damals?
Young people were very interested and active in politics. They thought about Socialism as a different political system.
Welche Auswirkungen hatte das auf die Gesellschaft?
Some of the protesters later became managers of big companies or banks. In spite of this, peace and environmental issues have become important topics in society.

31 *Musterlösung:*

Hello everybody
Jeremy is right. As there are more and more old people, young people should be given the right to vote so that we can take care that our interests are represented. There are a lot of young people who already work in youth councils and show interest in things concerning society. And besides, how can we learn about politics if we're not allowed to take part?

Das sollte in deiner Lösung enthalten sein:

- ☐ Du nimmst Bezug auf einige der bisher angesprochenen Punkte und Argumente.
- ☐ Du äußerst deine eigene Meinung und begründest sie.

Mögliche Pro-Argumente:
– young people want to decide certain issues
– they are interested in politics (e. g. school council or city youth council)
– some are members of political parties
– letting young people vote would be a way to interest them in politics
– young people might have to speak up for their issues as the proportion of older people is growing

Mögliche Contra-Argumente:
- young people are not interested in politics
- they only want to have fun
- they are not serious about political issues and don't care about society
- young people don't have the necessary knowledge and are influenced too easily

32

1. Could you be more careful, please?
2. Do you really think it's appropriate to talk to children like that?
3. I'd really appreciate it if you could not talk quite so loudly / talk a bit more quietly, please.
4. Would you mind closing the window, please?
5. I really don't think it's fair to take all the biscuits.
6. Stop laughing at him. That's not fair.
7. Please talk to her politely. It's not her fault.

Green Line

Die Trainingsbücher – passgenau zum Schulbuch üben!

ISBN 978-3-12-929894-7

ISBN 978-3-12-929896-1

ISBN 978-3-12-929976-0

ISBN 978-3-12-929982-1

ISBN 978-3-12-949162-1

Verbtabellen von A-Z – Alle Verben für sechs Schuljahre.

ISBN 978-3-12-926076-0

ISBN 978-3-12-926056-2

kompaktWissen – Die Schulbuch-Grammatik immer griffbereit!

Diese und weitere Klett-Lernhilfen sind im Buchhandel erhältlich.
Weitere Informationen unter **www.klett-lerntraining.de**

Alle Produkte passend zum Schulbuch

Die Vokabel-Lernboxen – Vokabeln lernen leicht gemacht.

ISBN 978-3-12-924008-3

ISBN 978-3-12-924013-7

ISBN 978-3-12-924022-9

Grammatik eines Schuljahres - immer griffbereit zum Nachlesen und Wiederholen

ISBN 978-3-12-926061-6

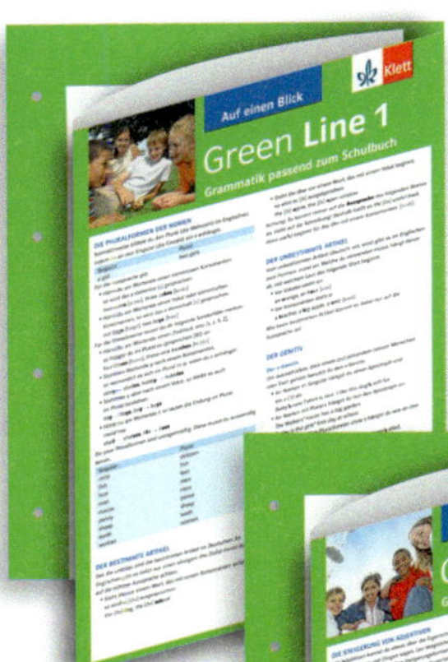

ISBN 978-3-12-926063-0

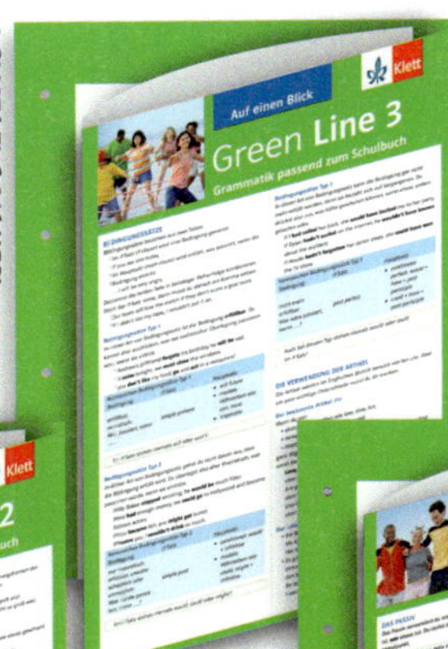

ISBN 978-3-12-926085-2

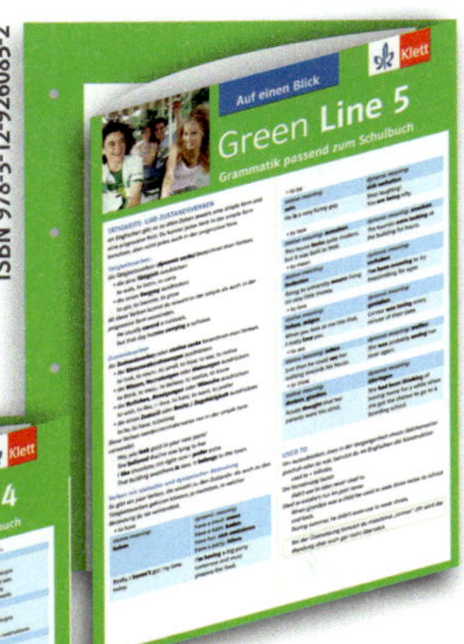

ISBN 978-3-12-926062-3

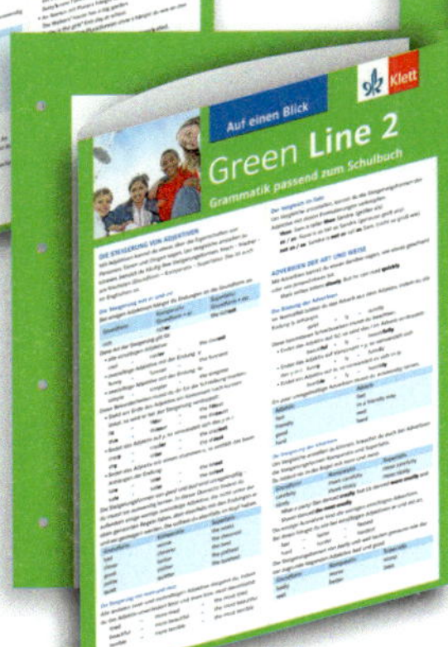

ISBN 978-3-12-926064-7

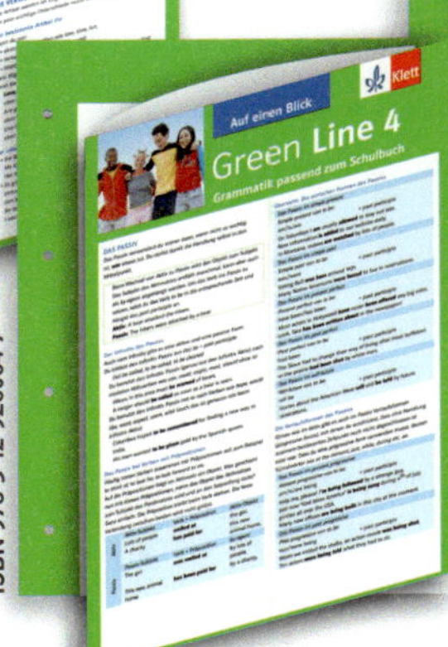